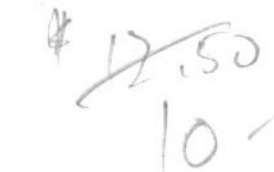

Organized by the
La Jolla Museum of Contemporary Art

LEO RABKIN
WORKS

La Jolla Museum of Contemporary Art
October 3–November 15, 1981

Dimensions are in inches: height, width, depth.

Unless otherwise noted, all works are Courtesy of Marilyn Pearl Gallery, New York.

La Jolla Museum of Contemporary Art
700 Prospect Street
La Jolla, CA 92037

Library of Congress Catalog Number: 81-83642
ISBN: #0-934418-11-X

Cover and page 1: *Tossed Thoughts in a Caribbean Villa*

Table of Contents

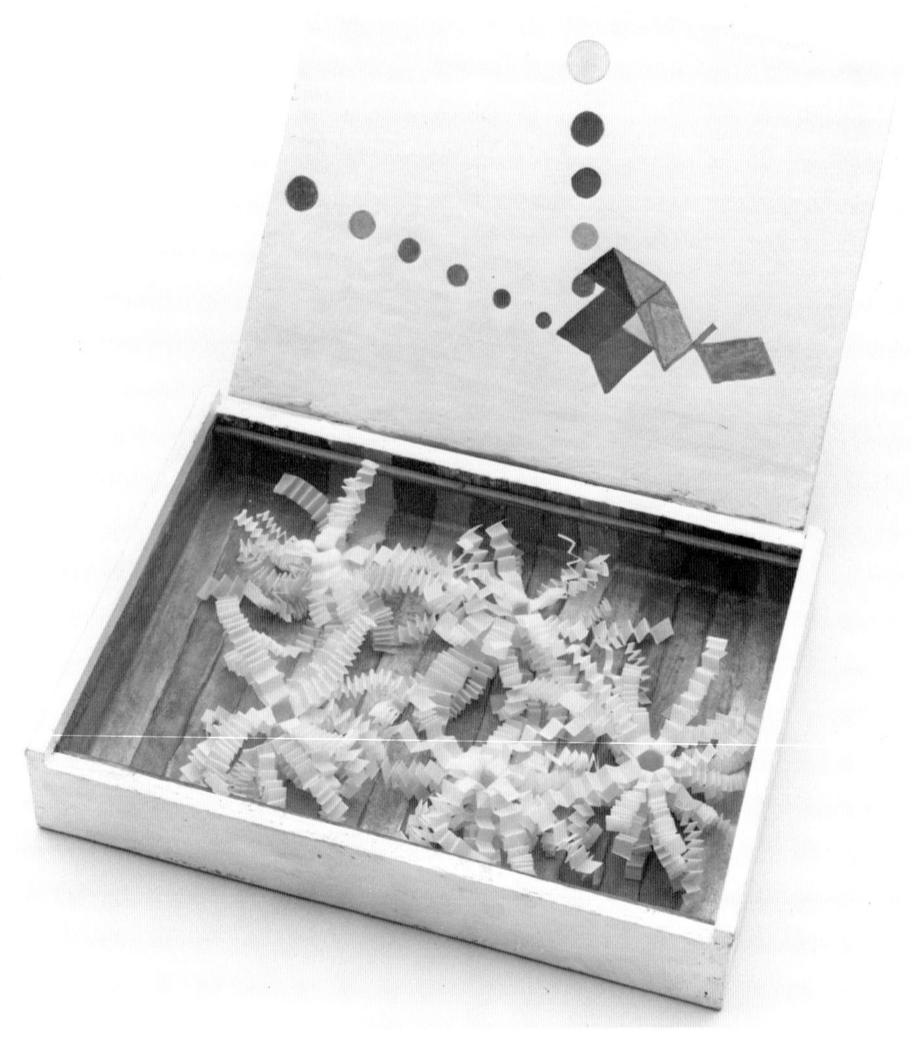

70 AAA—5 STAR, 1981
1¾ x 9¼ x 6½

Foreword

I have long been acquainted with Leo Rabkin's works and through my interest in his boxes and watercolors I became acquainted with the artist himself. Knowing him as a person has enriched my appreciation of what he does as an artist. When I speak of Leo, I also mean Dorothy Rabkin, his wife, for she not only is involved with him in his day-to-day life and in collecting examples of American primitive art, she is also intimately involved in his art as the first person who sees his works while he makes them and is their first critic.

Rabkin's luminous, color-saturated watercolors, although modest in scale, are assertive and require a lot of viewing space. They have that undefinable quality that we call "presence." His boxes, in contrast, are playful objects that stimulate the imaginations of adults as toys stimulate the imaginations of children. Rabkin's boxes are not in the tradition of toys, however. Their antecedents are Dada,[1] Marcel Duchamp[2] and Surrealism.[3] Having found a box to use, Rabkin fills it with a variety of objects and materials that evoke unconscious associations. These intimate sculptures also link Rabkin to artists like Paul Klee,[4] Kurt Schwitters,[5] Max Ernst[6] and Joseph Cornell.[7] The strongest influences on him, however, have not been art history or contemporary developments. His sources are his own life, beginning with his childhood in Cincinnati and continuing with his career in New York, and the example of American primitive artists, for their inventiveness and whimsy.

This is Leo Rabkin's first solo exhibition on the West Coast, and I feel that it is a privilege that this museum should have organized it. Chief Curator Robert McDonald worked in close collaboration with Leo and Dorothy Rabkin, and we are grateful for their many hours of painstaking effort. We are grateful, too, for the cooperation of the artist's New York representative, Marilyn Pearl.

Sebastian J. Adler
Director

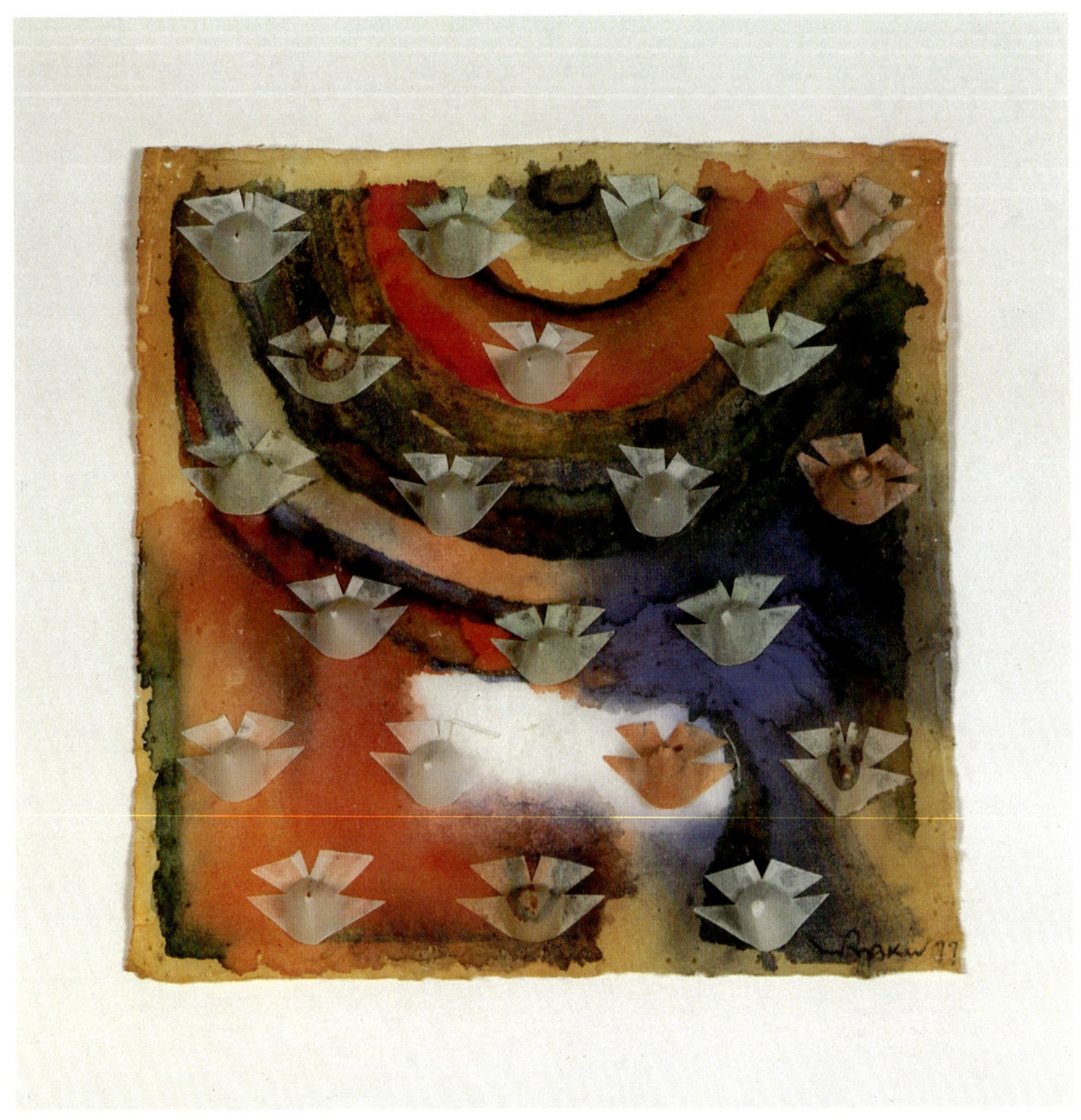

56 FLIGHT OF THE GEESE, 1977
6 x 6

Acknowledgments

Director Sebastian J. Adler initiated this exhibition and assigned me the responsibility for organizing it. From the very beginning his enthusiasm and support have enhanced the experience and facilitated the process.

One of the privileges enjoyed by curators of contemporary art is the opportunity to work with living artists. Leo Rabkin and his wife Dorothy have made this an especially satisfying undertaking, and I am grateful to them.

Among the Museum staff I want especially to acknowledge the participation of former Curatorial Secretary Mary C. Riley, who, with the assistance of Modern Art Council volunteer Vada Holsinger and Interns Linda Speer (graduate student, San Diego State University) and Anne Streicher (recent B.A., University of California, Los Angeles), verified the catalogue list and exhibition records. Anne Streicher also researched and wrote the footnotes. Intern Elizabeth Topper (graduate student, University of California, Los Angeles) assisted with the bibliography, and Intern Theodore Kingsley (graduate student, Emory University) prepared a useful summary history of the box in art as preparation for my introduction. Assistant Curator/Registrar Lynda Forsha and Assistant Registrar Bolton Colburn as usual performed their duties in an exemplary manner, as did Public Relations Officer Prudence Hutshing. Mark Williams typed early versions of the manuscript, and Marjorie Bobb prepared the final copy. Building Superintendent Michael Golino and Chief Preparator Robin Bright once again employed their gifts as artists to find creative solutions for the installation of Rabkin's unusual works.

It was a pleasure also to work again with designer Lilli Cristin, who combines practical good sense with high artistic standards. The representatives of Spectrum Printing (San Diego), especially John Woodrow and Tom Radke, again deserve our thanks for their skills and services.

Robert McDonald
Chief Curator

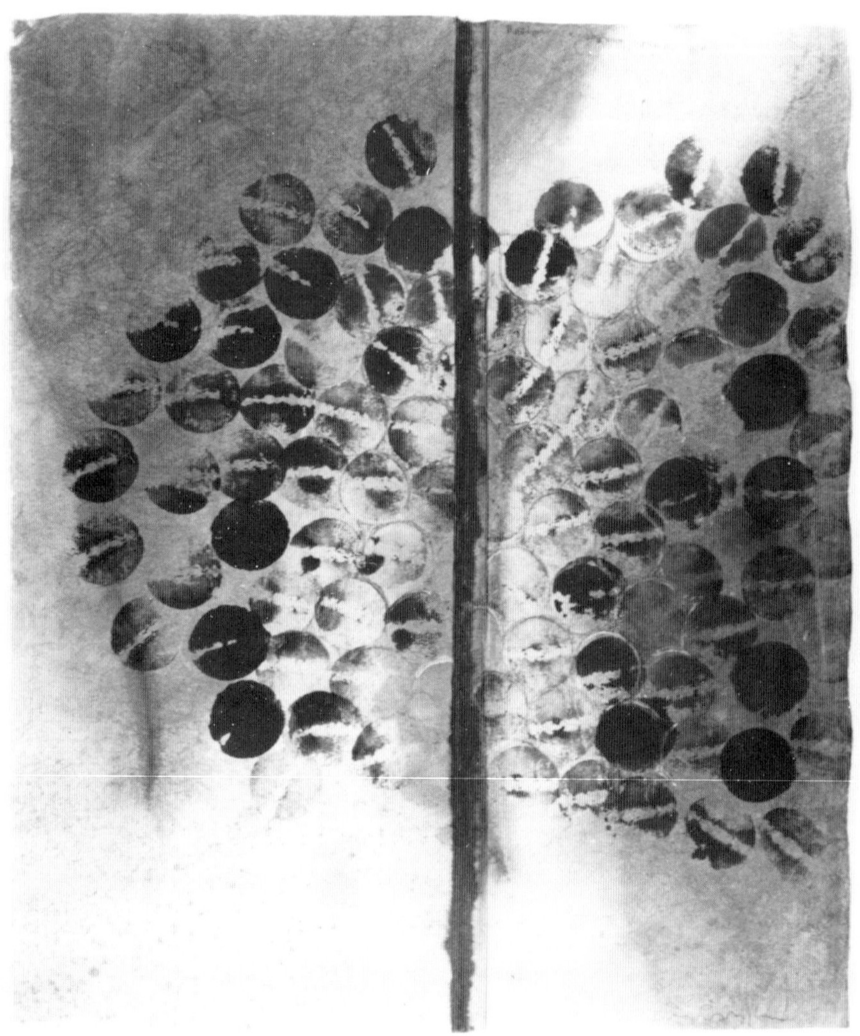

27 STAMPED AND CREASED (ORANGE FLOCKED LINE), 1970
7¾ x 6⅝

Introduction

Leo Rabkin is a romantic. In his appearance. In his lifestyle. In his attitudes. And in his works, which are images of himself.

Rabkin is a dandy, affecting the berets and neckerchiefs of a bygone bohemia. He lives with his wife Dorothy and their terrier, Billie Holiday, in a self-created cloister in Manhattan filled from floor to ceiling with works of art—his own, those of friends (renowned and not), and a large collection of American folk art. He is a voluble speaker whose enthusiasms propel him from subject to subject seemingly erratically because poetically, rather than rationally, interconnected.

He is romantic, too, in his aloofness from others, a characteristic dating from his youth. His family in Cincinnati was so large that no matter where he went he was certain to encounter at least a cousin. This very largeness, however, created a familial tolerance of difference that allowed Rabkin to develop as an individual. Yet it was this Russian-Jewish milieu with its respect for music, literature and theater that first stimulated Rabkin's interest in art and thus shaped the child which became the artist.

As a counselor and teacher of disturbed children in New York City schools, including several years in the area of Manhattan called "Hell's Kitchen," Rabkin performed his duties responsibly and compassionately. His artistic imagination was a source for solutions to urgent classroom problems, and encounters with those problems honed his improvisatory skills as an artist. He was not a time-server but a man engaged in his work. And yet, when he left the school building, he separated himself from the cares of the job and took up those of art.

Rabkin's romantic view of the artist as one who is destined to struggle alone in creating his art has precluded his involvement in groups. He remains on the periphery of the New York art scene. He has never been able to commit himself to an art movement or even philosophy in any sense other than the most general, specifically to abstraction.

In the realm of professional and political commitments, Rabkin is also independent. For decades he has been occupied with encouraging the acceptance of abstract art and with the problems of art as a profession, especially through the agency of American Abstract Artists, of which he is a past president. In the tradition of his family he is an active citizen guided by what he perceives as achievable, albeit not ideal, ends. Nevertheless, he neither enlists in causes nor signs manifestoes.

Although singular in his art, Rabkin is not a loner in the art world. He and Dorothy lead an active, albeit selective, social life, and throughout his career Rabkin has had close friendships with major figures such as Richard Lindner and Ad Reinhardt (both referred to in the Interview), among many others.

Rabkin centers his existence in his studio-home—formerly an iron foundry—in the Chelsea area of New York. The residence is entered from the street at ground level through a narrow storm door that opens into a narrow hall. To the left the visitor seemingly pops through another small door—as if in a Wonderland experience—into a large, high-ceilinged, skylighted, rectangular space. The tiny entry way psychologically permits control of what is allowed to enter, and the expansiveness of the space permits a filtering and diffusing of what might otherwise be intrusive influences. It is a quiet and separate space with soft light, a type of sanctuary. A counterbalance is the visceral charm of the country kitchen, located upstairs and beyond the studio more deeply recessed within the city block and away from the street, Dorothy's realm.

Although he and Dorothy lead a sequestered existence in their home, the source of Rabkin's art, beyond the content of his life, beginning with his boyhood in Cincinnati, and the stimulus of his imagination, is the city itself. For Rabkin New York is the most important place in the world because it is the most intense, the most unreal, the most artificial, the most magical. This microcosm of the world's peoples, cultures, religions, economies, politics and arts, this epitome of contemporary urban life with its glories and its problems nourishes Rabkin spiritually and materially. He distills its intense life into his works and discovers his materials in its streets and shops.

Rabkin's two bodies of works, watercolors and boxes, may be described as his formal and his informal works of art. The color-saturated watercolors are in the tradition of modern abstraction—but they are distinctively Rabkin's because of their facture, including their accordion-like pleats, which energize the lycricism of the horizontal bands of color. Their verticality relates to the stance of the artist and of the viewer and, tenuously, to the character of the urban environment. The materials are traditional, although exotic. Preparation for working on them involves almost ritualistic-like procedures and concentration, and, once engaged, the artist, because of the nature of the medium, must press through to a conclusion. Even the most subtly hued watercolors command attention. And they demand space. They attract as fire attracts, and yet they are, like their creator, aloof, emblems of an ideal art, reduced to color and line.

Whereas the watercolors represent Rabkin's creativity in its modern formal aspects, in historical antecedents, materials, and procedures, the boxes represent the artist informally, even intimately. Boxes are enclosed spaces related to buildings and architecture, although usually functional on a smaller scale. In making them, Rabkin joins an ancient tradition, for from pre-history to the present, folk artists, master craftsmen, sculptors and painters have adapted this utilitarian object to aesthetic ends. Spent by the deep concentration and intense physical control demanded by his watercolors, Rabkin turns to his boxes for release, for another kind of activity, a recreation. He fills them with materials selected from the environment, scraps of plastic, bits of paper, seeds and pods, and so forth. Most often his procedure is that of a tinkerer. He can take up a box, work on it, dismantle it, rework it, put it away, then return to it years or even a decade later. Similarly, visitors may pick them up and activate them, initially casually. Then their imaginations, memories and feelings respond, and the boxes work their magic. In the boxes Rabkin relates most clearly to the naive artists whose works make up his and Dorothy's collection of American folk art, and in them the boy from Cincinnati expresses himself along with the mature artist trained in New York.

Robert McDonald
Chief Curator

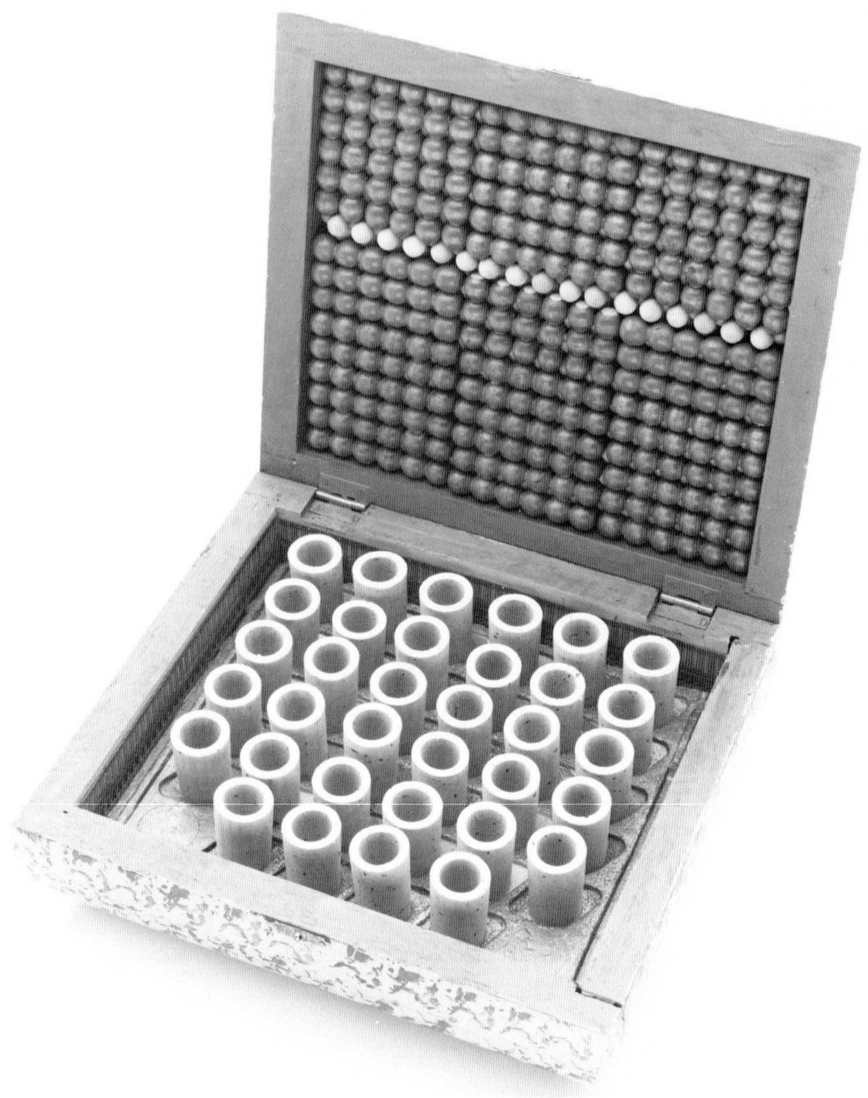

81 RUNNELS, THOUGHTS VEERING, 1981
3½ x 10 x 9

Artist's Statement

Over the past thirty years I have executed my "constructions" for my own studio, where I have tucked away each completed box in a jam or spice cabinet, a dough-trough, or a trunk, in pigeonholes of a salvaged country postoffice, or in other nooks and crannies. Until recently I felt the constructions would never be exhibited publicly, since they really cannot be conceived of as items for display. A special group has been selected for this exhibition. Ideally, the viewer encounters each construction, uncovers and holds it in the hands, turning and tilting it for changes in the light and activating the moveable parts. Although it is impossible to duplicate the same reactions in a public setting, I hope the observer of this exhibition will make every effort to simulate such private viewing experiences; for under the best of conditions the observer should feel alone, unhampered by time and filled with anticipation of the mystery surprise that comes from each unpredictable box.

Because they are intended as visual surprise-encounters for an audience-of-one, I refer to my constructions as "discoveries." A fine setting for them would be an attic or a cellar—the lighting unfavorable, the temperature extreme, the odors pungent, and all the senses of the viewer keyed high for the soul to soar into long-familiar reaches. The result should be a discourse between the viewer and the construction, *provided* that the viewer frees himself of his learned metaphors and literal references and recovers from childhood the many non-rational, non-verbal, subliminal sensations that have no prejudicial references.

Today, when the state of contemporary art is at its most self-conscious (and is even abandoned by a counter-culture), I must continue to create for my private world and avoid special or intentional styles or interpretations. My work varies in composition, choice of materials and executions. The approach will range from the conceptual to the intuitive. Labels such as idea art, romantic, or abstract surrealism are avoided. I enjoy the luxury of diversification. On the other hand, I am aware that my work remains rigidly abstract. I would sooner search for a deeper poetical image than the superficial objective-subjective image. I leave much of what I do to be interpreted by others. But I hope that from the viewer's beginning nugatory experiences meaningful pleasures may develop.

Leo Rabkin
New York, 1981

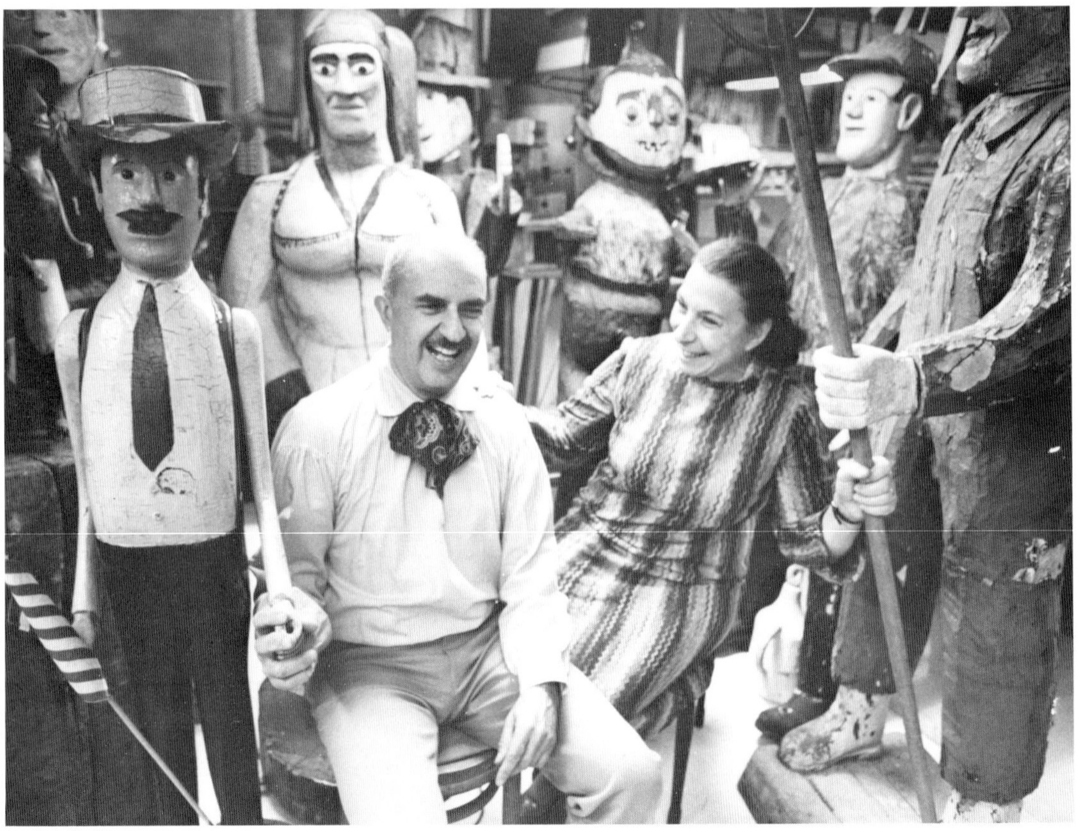

Leo and Dorothy Rabkin with part of their folk art collection (Photo courtesy of People Weekly)

A Conversation: Leo Rabkin, Dorothy Rabkin, and Robert McDonald[8]

RM Leo, anyone who sees your work asks why you use boxes.

LR I think of them as symbolic of the most personal, precious and powerful things that we have. Kids have boxes for their most secret treasures. And in school, too, we all had our little boxes—pencil boxes, lunch boxes, cases for our art supplies. They were part of our means of organization. As time went on I began to realize how many people collect and *love* boxes. I think this goes back to when we were children, and it never leaves us.

RM Any number of writers have remarked about you that in making boxes you reveal the child in the adult.

LR Yes, but these boxes are not for children. A child's attention span is too brief. If a child has his own boxes, then it's another story. But a child cannot relate his experiences to anyone else's.

RM The child doesn't yet have a wealth of cultural references.

LR Yes, he hasn't gone through enough living. He doesn't have the memories. All that my boxes really do is trigger unconscious thoughts that the person is unaware of—reactions to texture, color, light, dark, shininess, anything. Who knows what's going to happen? When I give demonstrations I might present twenty boxes because I know with that many I can reach everyone. I would say that out of twenty, anyone would respond unconsciously to at least three.

To go back to your original question, Why do I make boxes? I make them because they bring me the most marvelous audience that I could not have any other way. I know that if they're intelligent or capable of forming images, I will be able to win them over somehow.

RM Who is the audience?

LR Anybody. They just have to be alert, and they have to be able to feel. There is something magical about opening a lid and discovering something unusual that causes an immediate reaction. They may be repelled by lots of things, and that may also be good. The psychological impact of the box is so important and overpowering that once that person relates to the box, I'm no longer in the picture. My personality is never in the exhibition, and I enjoy that, too.

RM To me the boxes have the same kind of intensity that you find in very brief poems.

LR That's the thing. I have been mostly influenced by Gaston Bachelard.[9] He is my bible. He's a phenomenologist. He uses poetry to explore what he calls "the poetics of space." He uses Rilke[10] and Mallarmé.[11] By the way, I am not a frustrated writer. I didn't think I ever had the talent, and I never found that discipline. I love poetry, but I can't write at all. The boxes are the nearest thing to that sort of expression, and that's why I like Bachelard so much. Just look at the table of contents in *The Poetics of Space:* 1 The House. From Cellar to Garret. The Significance of the Hut; 2 House and Universe; 3 Drawers, Chests and Wardrobes; 4 Nests; 5 Shells; 6 Corners; 7 Miniature; 8 Intimate Immensity; 9 The Outside and Inside; 10 The Phenomenology of Roundness.

RM Bachelard has more or less given you an intellectual justification for what you were already involved in.

LR Yes. And fortitude.

RM Yes. But you were already involved in doing something. Why were you doing that?

LR There are many reasons having to do with so many different things. Going back to the beginning, as a child, for example, I would save little shells, and I would glue them together on cards and paint them and put them in a box. Also when I was a kid I would make little sculptural things and keep them in a box. As time went on, I became involved in theatre. From age thirteen on I used to usher in Cincinnati, and I would see a performance every week. I loved it! And the theatre is a box. I played the violin, and the violin is a box, and it had a case—or a box. We always had a cellar, and we always had an attic, which are big boxes. Those are important considerations for any child's development.

RM That may be true, but not everyone is conscious of them to the degree that you are.

LR Apparently not. My mother was a great cellar gatherer, and so was my father. We also had a garage that we cleared out every year, and we also had attics in old houses with old trunks that had been abandoned.

RM You and Dorothy, I feel, have created a sort of box environment right here in your home. It's basically a long, high-ceilinged, rectangular space furnished with things precious to you, your collection of Shaker[12] chairs, works of art representing different phases of your development, and, of course, your collection of American folk art.

LR That's true. Richard Lindner[13] said, "Leo, you've moved in here and you wouldn't even know you're in Manhattan."

RM The furnishings have the qualities of the objects you put into your boxes.

LR Yes. If you look around, even upstairs in the kitchen, we have so many cabinets, but they're not the usual cabinets for a kitchen. They're little Shaker chests, or this or that. The folk art is very important.

RM How did you get started collecting it?

LR I had an uncle and cousins who were very big antique dealers. While I was going through college I would work for them in the summer. It was one of the best jobs I ever had. I rummaged around and picked up things. American folk artists used an enormous number of boxes in whatever they did. They had chests for feeding the animals. And they had boxes for keeping their tools. The women had baskets and boxes for their needlework. If you ever look around in a true 18th-century kitchen, there are all these little things. They had chairs that turned into boxes, and they had tables that turned into boxes. An awful lot of boxes. I love boxes. Due to folk art I had collected an enormous number of boxes, and I started using them. But I noticed the boxes became more and more expensive. You don't need valuable objects to really reveal your feelings. I just decided I was going to stick to old boxes that cost a quarter, or a dollar at the most, and that everything that went into the box must have no value either, and that was the fun. I'm not a lost-found object person, however. That's just not up my alley at all. I resent how people use feathers, and I resent how people use sand, because they've been used so brilliantly before. And it's totally misused, and it's aborting something. You should find any object. To find an object is just like going to the store and buying an object. You're finding them. You're selecting something. And if it has a certain visual feeling, I put it away. I have all these little boxes filled with things by categories. As long as they aren't expensive and not show-offy, and they don't have any particular meaning to anybody, then I keep them, and eventually I use them.

RM When you see a box you want to use, what's the kickoff for what you do? What is your procedure for making a work of art out of a box?

LR I don't know. I just do this and that. I took strawberry boxes, and they were a marvelous experience for me because every shape was exactly the same, all cubes or almost. It became a wonderful experience for me to have variations on a theme. I had an exact space that I was treating in different ways. I did several of them all in a matter of two weeks' time. Most of them. Others took many years' time. I see my biggest challenge as making three-dimensional sculpture with color. I think of Frank Stella,[14] for example, whom I admire because of his attempts to try to find the boldest, strongest colors that he can have and throw them into three-dimensional space. I think that with people like Stella you react either yes or no, because it's such strong stuff. It's amazing to see an artist using three-dimensional color, and I have always tried to do that.

RM What I'm trying to get at is how you decide what to start putting into a box. Do you run through the things you've collected, or what do you do? Is it intuitive?

LR Yes. It's never organized, rather totally disorganized. Downstairs I have two huge racks of boxes that are half-made. Some of them have been sitting there for fifteen years. Some have just been put there. I will start them, put them together and tear them apart, and not know what I'm doing. And—they're just fun!

Boxes are really an adjunct to my watercolors, or my watercolors are an adjunct to my boxes. I don't know which is what. When I do watercolors I cannot sustain myself over a period of time. I can do five or six watercolors and expect to have one or two fail. But if I should do ten, I might have six fail and then have three or four that I can keep. I get used up, so I immediately resort to the boxes, like doodles, like three-dimensional doodles. It's a matter of here's a space that's prescribed for me, and how do I fill it? And what do I fill it with? And I have hundreds of things that I can fill it with if I want to. But a hundred things are really overpowering, so I make an arbitrary decision and just stop right here. I have certain things I keep repeating that help me along, certain techniques like flocking. By now I have enough little techniques that I can always resort to so that I don't have to feel that I'm completely incapacitated. But on the other hand, I'm often at a loss because I have so many things that I can use I don't know what to use. It's boundless.

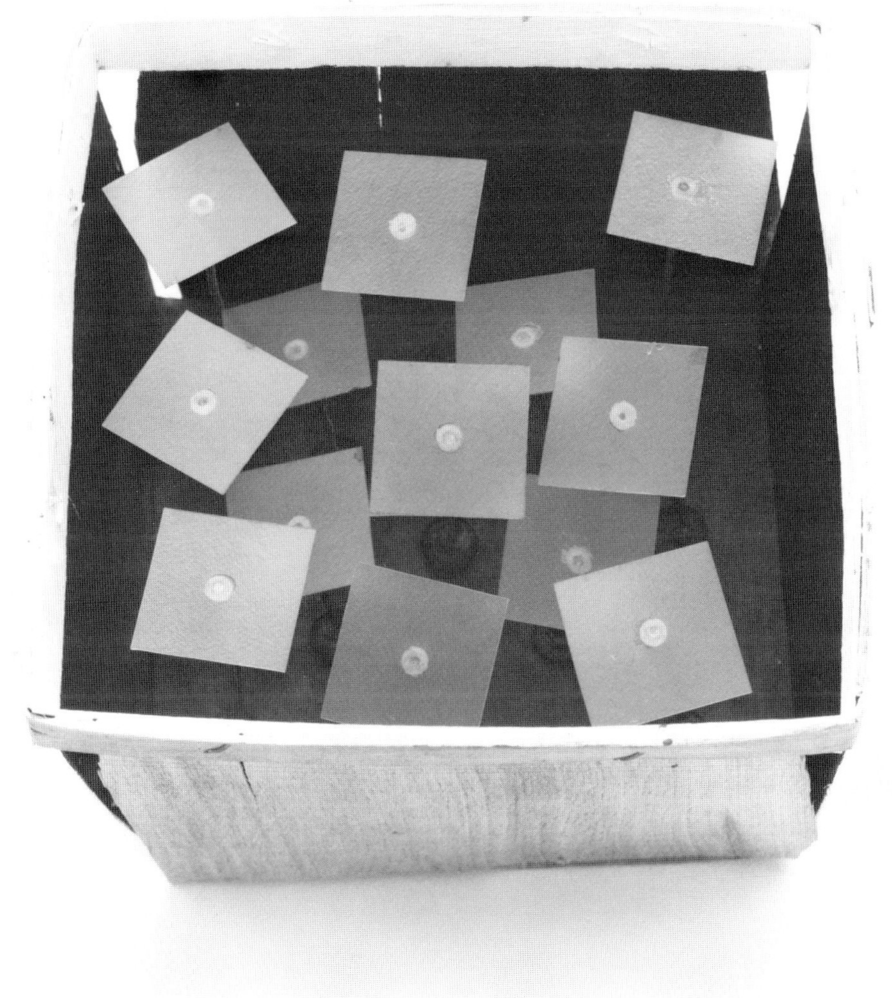

4-17 EIGHTEEN STRAWBERRY BOXES —
VARIATIONS ON A THEME
THIRTEEN UNSAFE SQUARES, 1979
3 x 5⅜ x 5⅜

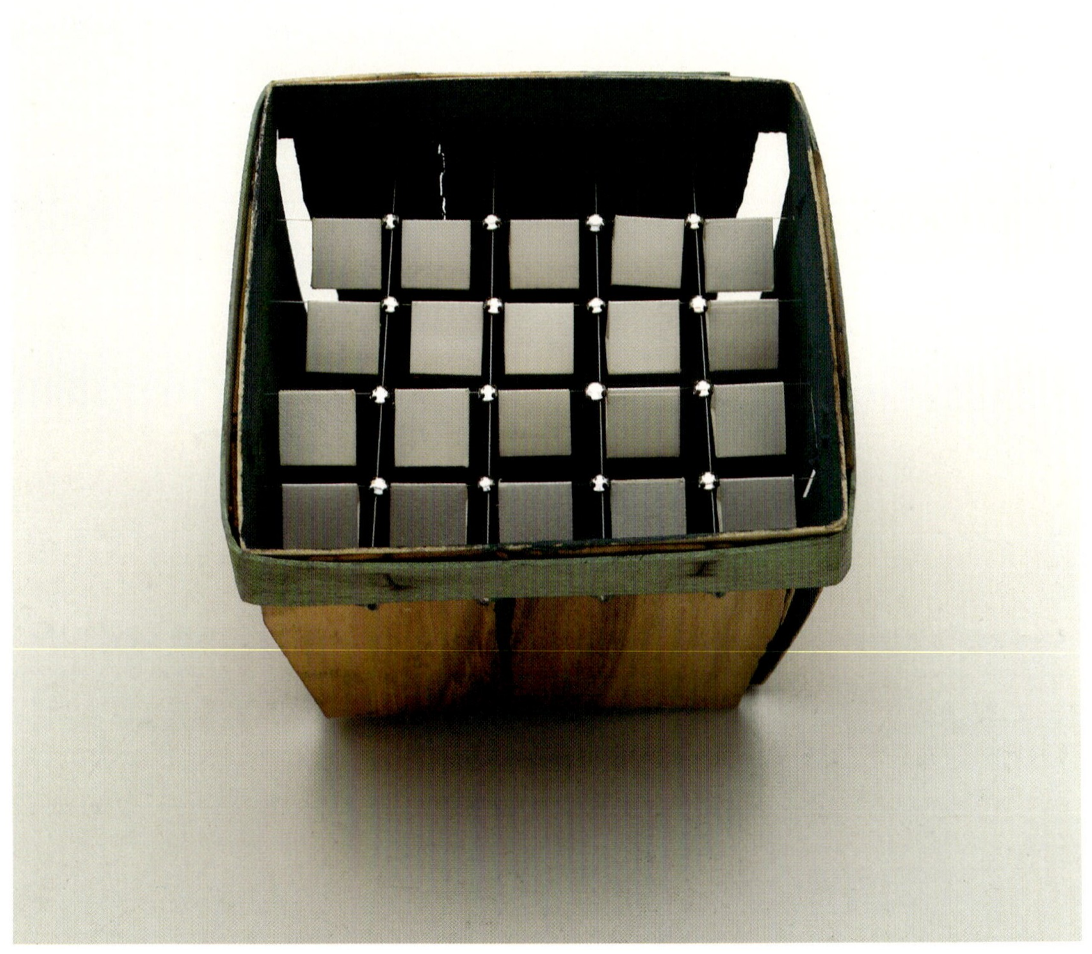

4-2 EIGHTEEN STRAWBERRY BOXES—
VARIATIONS ON A THEME
TWENTY NERVOUS TRIANGLES, 1960
2½ x 4¼ x 4¼

Is there a reason to save string? Dorothy and I went to a plastics show for merchants, and they were throwing away pieces of plastic. We gathered up bags and bags of these little findings. It was in the 1950's, and I still have many bags of these cast-offs.

But I don't arrange materials accidentally. People will see pilings in the water, and they'll exclaim, "Isn't that fantastic sculpture! Isn't it marvelous!" And I think it's very nice that you can look at the clouds and find horses and dogs or look at pilings in the water and see sculpture. There's a great ambiguity between what is an art form and what is not an art form.

I think it's a very big dilemma today. Everyone's looking for something to remind them of something. I like to see things that are nicely done, that's true. I like to see pilings in the water, but to call that sculpture is I think going a bit too far.

RM I agree, it's not *meant* as sculpture.

LR That's the reason, exactly. People say that's better than sculpture, but there's no *intention* to make art. Everyone is entitled to his own opinion about what he wants to call art. We're all so insecure as to what we really think and feel about art but that doesn't mean that we should then become subservient to the specialists or intimidated by people who don't know. It's very irritating to me.

RM Let's talk a moment about the scale of the boxes. They are very small, portable, all handable. I don't know how true this is in New York, but in California there is a very important movement toward miniaturization in art works.

LR I don't know about it now. Everything that I make has to be held in the hands. It's not fondling or caressing at all. It's just that it has to be intimate. I think of a child with a box. Because you can't experience a big thing. I don't want to have any of my things on a monumental scale.

I want them very, very intimate. A box has so much mystery to it when you're just looking at it, a psychological impact. But holding it in your hand is very nice and makes it accessible.

RM Another aspect of your work is that it's so rich in terms of content that evokes responses in whoever is holding the work, even though the individual elements are not necessarily laden with meaning.

LR That to me is very important. I am not looking for anything with a reference. These are not valuables. They're just paper or bits of plastic that have never been used before. I use them in a new context.

RM How do you relate the color you use in the boxes to your other work?

LR It's arbitrary. I get really fouled up on watercolors. Watercolors need sustained time. When I start a watercolor it keeps me standing one, two, three days. I really exhaust myself. Color is even harder with boxes, because they're three-dimensional. I mix my own color for watercolor but in the boxes I use anything, enamel paint, flocking, anything for the boxes. I will use almost anything, which I would never do with watercolors. The watercolors have a sort of purity that the boxes don't. The boxes don't require that much concentration. I can just stop making a box at any time and pick it up again. But a watercolor I have to go right through.

RM So the boxes are in effect a form of recreation. Do you consider that the watercolors are the more significant group of works?

LR I don't think so. I spend an enormous amount of time on the boxes. They are very time-consuming. Although they look like nothing they require enormous amounts of time. I hope they don't show it, though, too much. And I would like the watercolors to look like they were done in just two minutes.

RM They have that quality even though obviously it's painstaking work.

LR One thing about them that is very strange is that people who buy watercolors don't collect them as they do boxes. One watercolor suffices because it is so strong, but people like to have several boxes. I hope they don't become a commodity. I want people to have them because they give great pleasure. I don't want them to feel intimidated by the presence of my personality.

RM It makes you happy that the work becomes a personal possession.

LR Yes, it's no longer a commodity. And I don't think art should be a commodity.

RM That's an attitude that's different from other

artists who are concerned with their continuing interest in their works of art.

LR Transitoriness in art and mortality in life are things that don't scare me. That's why I admire artists like Yves Klein[15] and Christo.[16]

RM I sense that myself. Let's talk for awhile about the watercolors. They are extraordinarily beautiful and vibrant. Though relatively small in scale—a finished piece is how large? 25 by 25 inches?—they have a presence that demands a lot of space around them.

LR They should not be hung close to one another.

RM Tell me how you make these works, the kind of paper you use, the pigment, the procedure.

LR At first I used heavy English, Italian or French paper, but in drying the color faded away. Then I began using various thinner, Japanese papers. I enjoy its strength. I was also introduced by chance to Thai paper, which is finer. It's used for kites. It's handmade paper like tissue paper—enormously strong. You can see through it. It's almost transparent. The pigment is suspended on the paper. It's only when you hang it against a backing that it becomes opaque. That's very important. The paper requires a lot of preparation. I have plywood boards covered with plastic for a hard, smooth surface. I have a large collection of exotic brushes, mostly from China. And I grind my own colors, which is a painstaking process, but it's necessary for the dry quality that I want. I paint with very thick pigments to create the moth-like surface that I want. I can keep the paper moist by covering it with aluminum foil and before drying I tack a binding around the edges so it becomes taut.

My works definitely are not like Nolde's,[17] but I strive for his color. When you see a Nolde watercolor personally you are overwhelmed. I've gone through the palette as Nolde does using pure color. Maybe I'm praising him too much, but he's never given the credit he deserves. Other German Expressionists use brilliant color, but never as he did.

It is always Nolde who is the basis for my watercolors. He was one of the magnificent painters of flowers and landscapes. Of course, Dorothy is always in the background and a big influence on me. She is a great fan of Nolde's. I've always needed more encouragement with my watercolors than with my boxes. I didn't much care about my boxes. I just happened to think of that now... strange. I always know that someone will find two or three boxes they like. I am very impersonal about the boxes. I don't have any sense of possession of them.

RM You seem to be demanding in your editing of watercolors.

LR Very much so.

RM Working with the medium of watercolor is very difficult. The paper is almost like silk. If you make a mistake and can't incorporate it into what you are doing the whole thing is lost.

LR That's what I'm getting at. Sometimes watercolors take a day or more because things happen —I don't call them mistakes—but something I have to work out.

RM An analogy is life, where you do not have a second chance. It's simply an additive process.

LR You can't go back to correct things, that's true. Sometimes there's a marvelous happening. I plan and want to be certain about what happens, but things never happen to work out that way. That's why I like watercolor so much, because it's so stimulating. That's why I cannot do it much however, because it becomes exhausting.

RM Tell me about the folding process in watercolors.

LR I had been unconsciously folding paper and using it in my boxes for over twenty years. For some reason I took a watercolor and I folded it, and folding became the most important part of my watercolor. It provided an entire structure. I could then read it. It had become my work of art. It has many things to it. The three-dimensional things—shadow, depth—make it very intense, much more than if it were flat. The vertical lines sustain the composition.

RM It's the intensity that makes them require as much space as they do.

LR It becomes like a textile with the thickness of weaving. Unconsciously your eye goes in and out over the surface. The shadows give it depth, and the reflected colors give it intensity. With the pleating I don't have to worry about composition, because the vertical line is the composition.

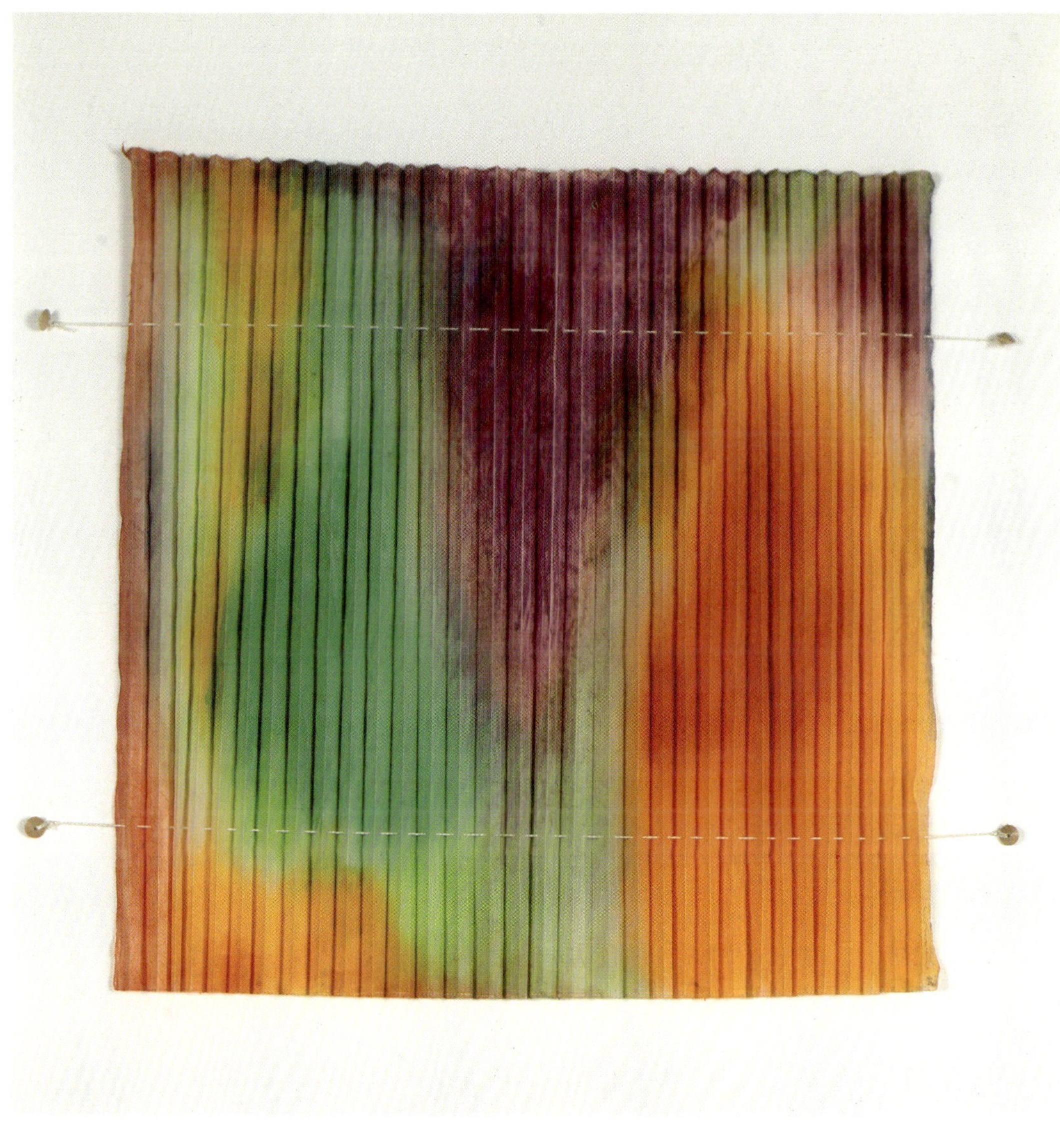

68 SECONDARIES, 1980
18 x 18 plus string

RM What you are doing now is combining very rich color with a reductive composition.

LR Yes.

RM You use the vertical lines of a grid. The composition is also horizontal, however, in the way you use the color. And the string and bead mounting device you use provide additional horizontal linear elements.

LR For years I was living in terror. I knew Ad Reinhardt[18] and Sol LeWitt[19] and all the minimalists. I was always surrounded by them. I got so I couldn't draw anything. I couldn't stand the grid. When things come on too heavy I cannot identify. I could not come out with a group statement. I was always aloof and remained very much alone. I have always been peripheral. It was always part of my whole picture. Dorothy and I are very, very private people in a very social way. In college I was always called the world's best friend, which has a double meaning. Because on the surface I got along with everybody. And my social skills were very adequate. But to become a bosom pal of anybody was out of the question, and I cannot identify with any particular group.

RM So you have a self-contained life.

LR Yes. I think every artist has his own world and his own way of going around. We are all so different. You have to face reality and adjust to everybody. On the other hand I just can't become a fanatic!

RM I want you to explain your feeling about the boxes having a kind of content that the watercolors don't have, their psychological content or referentiality.

LR The trouble with the watercolors was that I was always worrying about form. They substitute for all my anxieties about the watercolors. I do boxes because it's very pleasurable to me. It's humor. It's light. It's easy, although very time-consuming. Yet it's a distraction, which is psychologically a different type of thing.

RM What do you think people get out of boxes?

LR Once I do a box it is no longer mine. It's not my property anymore. It belongs to the person who has a reaction to it. Even if they hate it, I think it's terrific. I enjoy having the boxes presented to anybody and watch their reactions. After doing it for so many years an unfavorable reaction doesn't bother me because I know someone else will come along with a different imagination and some insight. I don't get upset and never will. The reactions of people toward the boxes are their own. I now feel I've done my job, and the rest can go on. There are some people whose lives are so depleted that they may have no reactions at all.

RM What are some of the formal art historical influences on you that you are conscious of?

LR There were a number. The most important influence has been the Germans, not the French, especially Klee and Grosz,[20] and Max Ernst, or actually any of the German Expressionists or Bauhaus[21] people.

RM I certainly see a relationship to Klee. I don't see a relationship to Grosz.

LR I think the influences are the surrealism of Ernst, the humor of Klee, and Grosz because he represented the German mentality and social consciousness. I was very much a part of that.

RM Many of the younger artists now are reacting against purely abstract art and putting content into their paintings, other than purely visual content. Some are using the figure along with an expressive line and form and narrative content.

LR I wish I could do that. I can't. It's a marvelous release to be able to do that. I am so much older. I just cannot do it that way. I am not young. Everything I do is much more delicate and tidy and compulsive. The compulsiveness that I maintain in my personality is of another period of time. I am much more structured. I just couldn't go into other things. The problems in my art are artistic ones.

RM And yet, Leo, you are an active citizen. You are informed about political, social and economic problems, and you've been professionally active for a long time in American Abstract Artists.[22] Also as a teacher in the public school system in the slums, you've been on the front line.

LR Yes. But I didn't teach art. I kept those activities separate, mostly. Teaching didn't permit me to live in an ivory tower. I did a lot of unusual things in my work with kids new to the country. I had kids from Puerto Rico, or Harlem, or Bed-Stuy [Bedford-Stuyvusant, an area of Brooklyn]. I worked for seventeen years with very disturbed girls. They didn't care anything about my art. They were involved with themselves, and every day in their neighborhood they faced some physical threat, a bloody nose or a knifing. I would teach

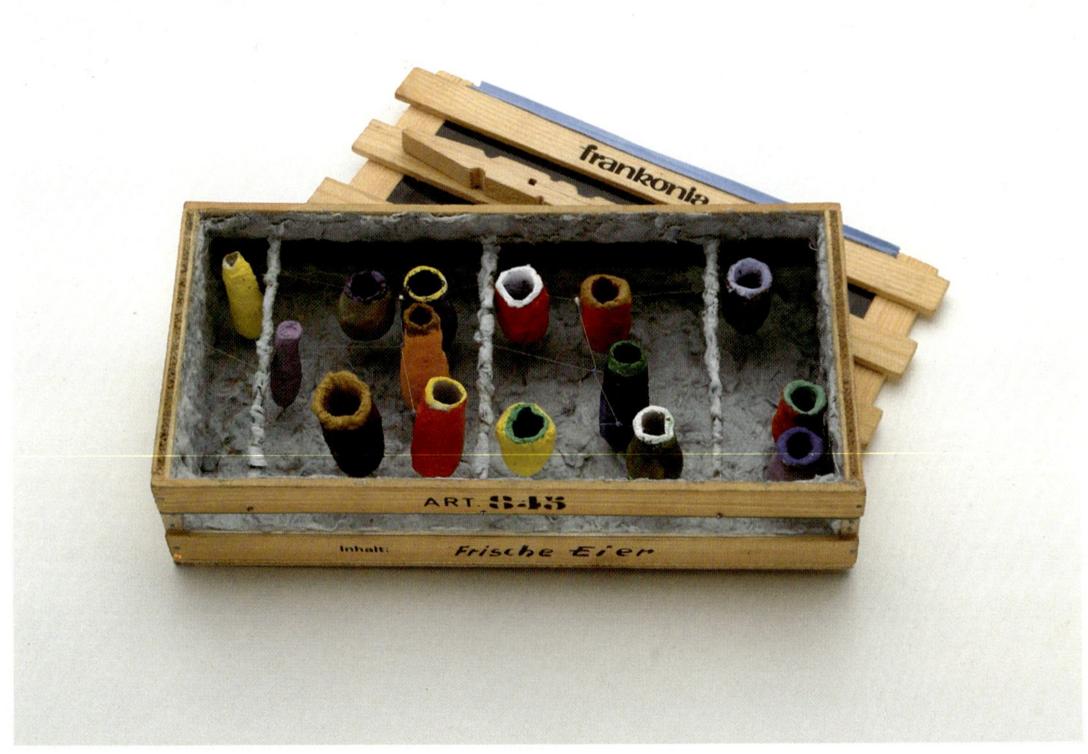

65 ART 345, FRISCHE EIER, 1980
2¾ x 8⅛ x 3¾

them the simplest activities, to read or type. Maybe teaching helped me in my art because I had to improvise all the time and make use of whatever opportunity I could find. Teaching was an honest and fulfilling job. After 2 P.M. I became another person. As an artist I think you have to find your own world.

RM Do you think it's possible to teach art?

LR For some people yes. Not for me. Over the years I have developed my own personal thing that I don't understand that well. I think that Klee must have been a wonderful teacher at the Bauhaus, but his book on teaching is overly pedantic. Cézanne[23] also preached one thing and executed another.

RM It seems that it is a mistake for an artist to try to explain what he or she does, in any but the most vague terms.

LR That's why I could not teach art, for that very reason. In addition, it becomes so stimulating I exhaust myself. When I face a group and try to state my ideas it is difficult because it is hard enough to know what I am doing at all.

RM Leo, to return to what you do, you also make pastels, in addition to watercolors and boxes.

LR Yes, and all the pastels are three-dimensional. I form the paper on an intaglio press to create a relief. For example I use rope to make an impression. I use certain forms or materials to give me a composition. After that I use pastels. I am also making experimental prints that are three-dimensional.

RM I wanted to ask what these beads on the watercolors are.

LR They're wood usually, for making jewelry. When I worked with girls at school I used them for motivation and to develop coordination. I made them do beadwork. Without much effort they had something of their own. Ownership is not for the slums. It was almost impossible for them to make a necklace and wear it without fear of it being ripped off. I discussed with them the idea of the calabash. It's a hollow gourd that people in primitive societies use for carrying things. It's like a box. If you live in violent neighborhoods you are not permitted to possess anything. But if you have a

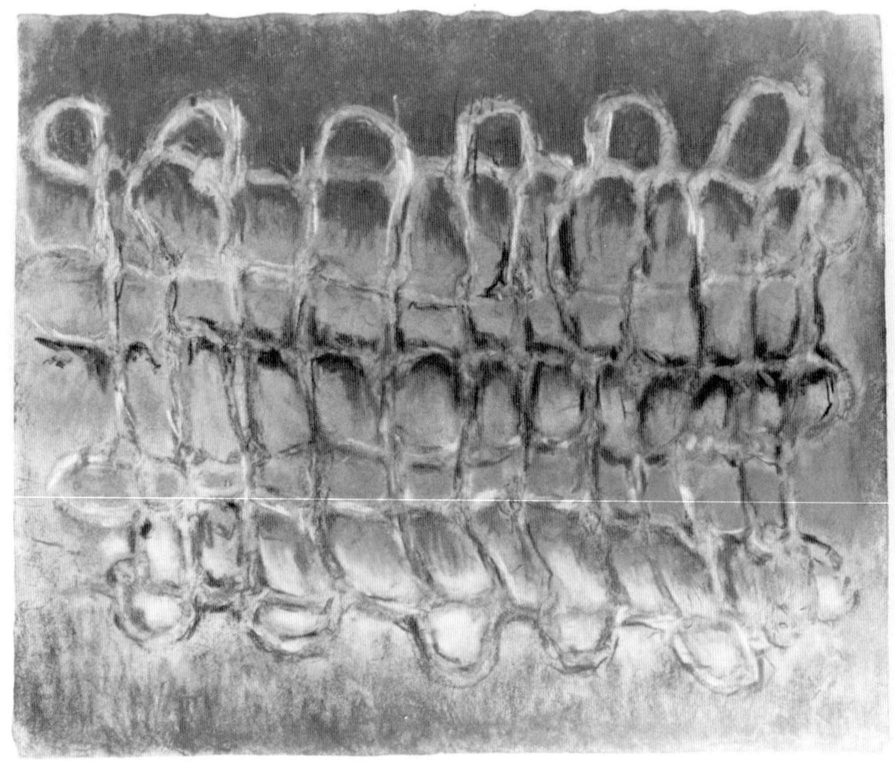

80 ROPE PASTEL IN PURPLE AND GREEN, 1981
10½ x 12½

little cigar box you can always carry it around with a few tiny possessions in it, then no one will get it.

RM In a sense, the total environment of New York has provided you with certain kinds of stimulation and materials that you use in your work.

LR Very unconsciously. I always worked with teenagers. You had to be very flexible and resort to anything you could do to maneuver a situation.

RM The kind of intimacy that is a characteristic of your work might be seen as a response to the indifference of the environment.

LR It's true. It is a protection... you're exposing yourself and also protecting yourself. I don't know where the boxes or watercolors start. Things suddenly burst open or are collected together.

RM You've said, "Dorothy is very much my eyes."

LR Yes. She is actually my critic. We don't have groups for critiques, so I am very fortunate to have Dorothy. She is the single person I resort to. It's quite amazing how much I rely on her. She has an enormous facility for connecting things. She has a specialized ability which she uses frequently in her thinking and an unusual eye. Few people can do this. She always connects things with something seemingly unrelated. She reacts emotionally to art and not intellectually.

RM Other than going to museums and living with you, she has had no formal art training, is that correct?

LR But she was interested in oriental art before we were married.

[Dorothy Rabkin joins the conversation.]

LR We were talking about you. I said that you were not educated in art in terms of formal education. On the other hand, you had a very sophisticated background from your parents in Germany.

DR I always was, even as a child, seeking out art. My father took my sisters and me to museums in Berlin. He was more interested in three-dimensional art than in two-dimensional. He didn't go to museums to see the paintings as much as he went to see especially Greek sculpture. He also liked primitive art in the Museum of Natural History. After the war [World War II, 1939–1945] I had a "boyfriend" who was an art collector. He gave me a fantastic education in art. His great love was art, especially German Expressionism. After the war was over, because I didn't have any education, I couldn't take up formal studies, but I went to Berlin University and I sat in on lectures, especially on German literature and on art. As a book dealer I found myself specializing in books illustrated with engravings and lithographs.

RM Why did you become involved in American folk art, which is very different from a European tradition?

DR Because it was free, not bound to tradition. It was not European. We always had the order, even in school when we had art. Even when we had art lessons at school we had to learn to do everything in proportion. God forbid if we didn't use proportion or convention as was expected! This is why folk art appeals so much to me, it was not bound to tradition and no one cares for proportion. Just what came to the minds and what mood they were in, what materials they had in hand. People made use of the freedom they had in this country.

What also impressed me when I was a very young teenager was a show of degenerate art.[24] I saw it and had never seen anything like that before in my life. It made an enormous impression on me. Especially Paul Klee. I couldn't get over it. Then I came to America after the war, and it was terribly lonesome. I was just completely lost here. The people my sister and I stayed with were so uncultured, so... I went to the Museum of Modern Art and I walked into a room, and there was the Paul Klee "Twittering Machine" I had admired so much as a young girl during that show. From that moment I didn't feel like a stranger anymore. It was like coming home.

RM I think you're the only one I have ever been acquainted with personally who saw that exhibition, which is so famous.

DR It was fantastic! The most impressive thing was the comments they had next to each painting. What somebody had paid, how many thousands of marks. I couldn't believe these marvelous things were being called degenerate, because they were so fantastic to me. The show was a real eye-opener. Now when you go to Germany you don't see anything else but this art. The galleries are full of it.

RM I have wondered if any other people who went through that exhibition received any education.

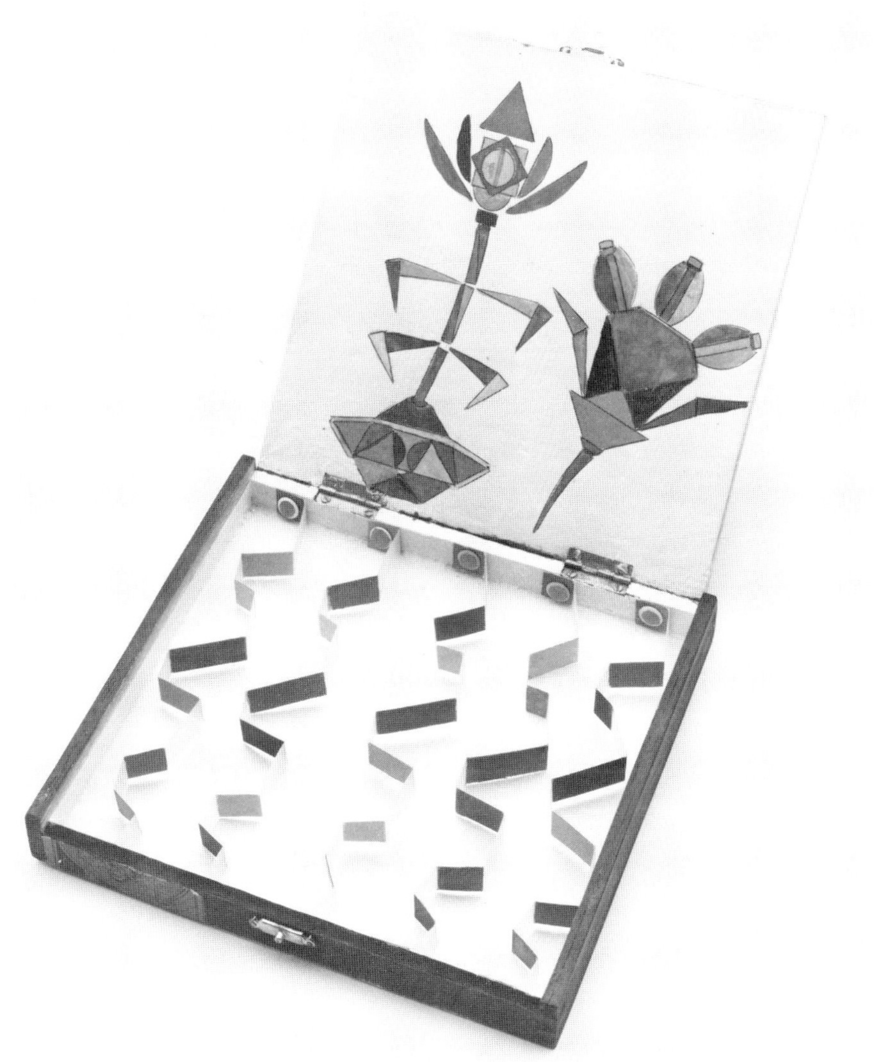

76 PARA TOBACOS TORCIDOS, 1981
1 x 7⅛ x 7½

DR It's unbelievable how many thousands went through that show, and I think most of them who went there were more interested than against it.

RM I don't doubt that. Leo has said that you act as his eyes. How do you interpret that?

DR As his eyes and through constructive criticism. Sometimes I just tell him what I am thinking he should do with something before he even goes into it. [To Leo] Don't I?

LR Absolutely true. If I am able to override anything she says, then I am convinced I am able to do it. That makes the conviction much stronger. If I cannot, then I will listen to her. I give her credit for helping me.

RM Yes. What kind of criticism do you make?

DR Sometimes he has a tendency to do too much and I always tell him.

RM You mean he overworks?

DR Overworks, tends to put too much, gets too busy, [To Leo] I hope you don't mind. I tell him less is more.

LR You do get lost, you know. That is always the problem of art. No one knows when to stop.

RM It could be said, as you are Leo's eyes, he is your hands. Is that possible?

DR To a certain extent, yes. It gives me great pleasure to be at least a little part of it.

RM Leo, you've said you never felt able to join a group or commit yourself to any kind of group.

LR I am aloof. I think it's amazing that Dorothy and I have known so many famous artists and critics, not that we have made an effort to know them, we were just lucky to have met them. But they were never a group.

RM The point I am trying to get to you is that you really didn't need that group because you had Dorothy—Dorothy is your group.

LR Actually a sounding board. Everyone has to have one I guess.

DR I reacted to his art from the very first time I was in his studio. I think he was painting this one [an early torn painting]. I was breathless. I thought it was fantastic. At that time he had to take a lot of abuse from certain people who couldn't get used to the idea that he had to slash the canvas. I really thought it was fantastic.

RM Earlier I commented to Leo I thought of his work as a defense—the intimacy of the work, the scale and feeling as a statement against the environment of New York.

DR I don't feel that way. I always feel he is very outgoing but at times shy.... He never reveals himself completely even to me or anybody.

RM So there's always some mystery. [To Dorothy] Leo said you had an extraordinary eye.

DR Yes. It is like something pulling me over, this magnet. When I see something that's interesting or good I feel I have to have that or look at it and then sometimes I have a feeling that I have seen it somewhere else and it usually turns out that I was right. I have a good memory.

RM It is an intuitive thing, but it involves practice, too. A friend once was asked, How do professionals evaluate art? How do you get to the point of saying this is good or this is bad? She replied that through practice you compile a personal slide library that you flip through in your head.

DR I know of course interest and knowledge and love for art play a part. I know of all the children at home I was the only one who loved to go to the museums. The most important thing is to have a certain emotional reaction to a thing you see. □

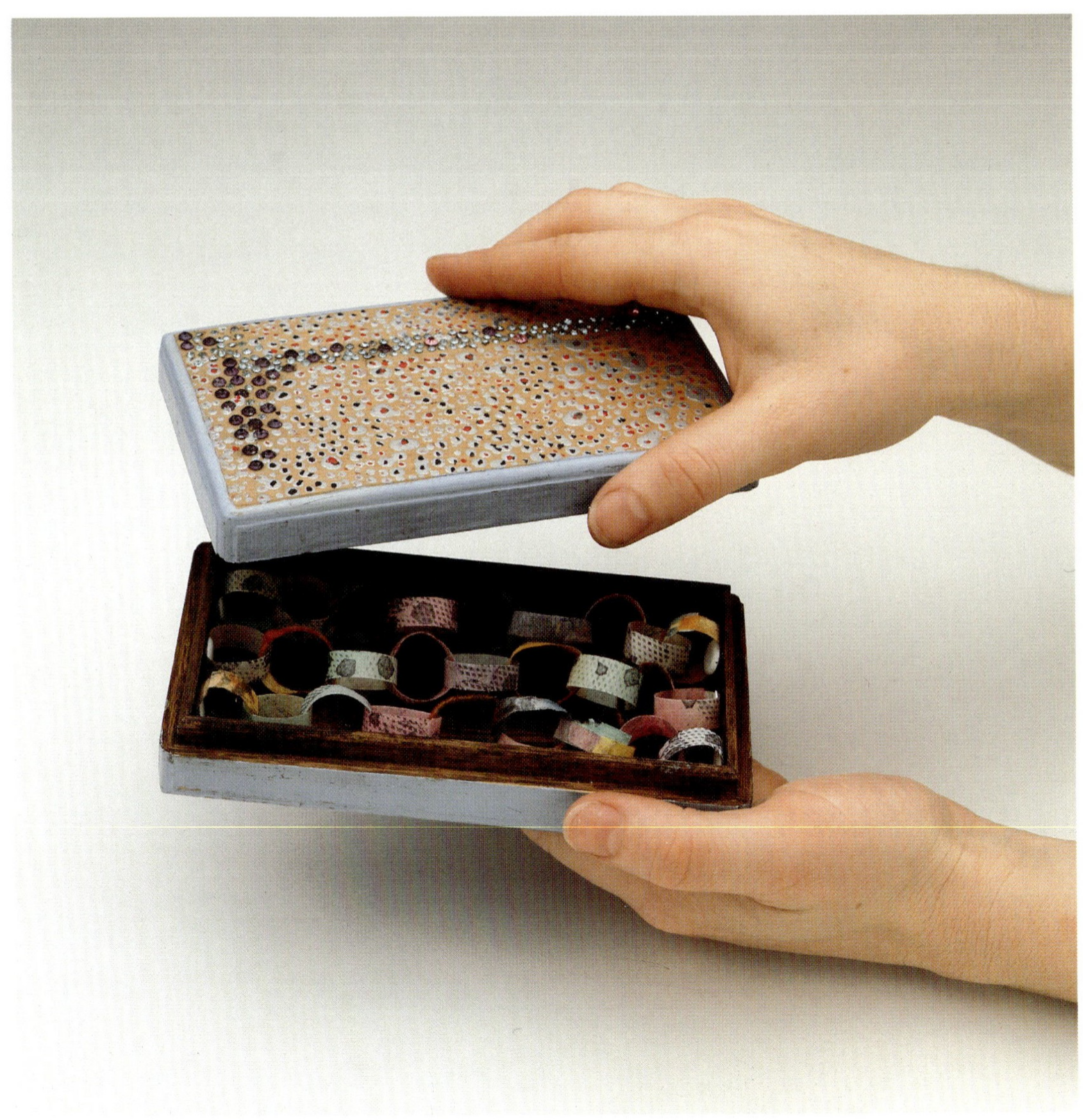

34 KINDERGARTEN ART NOUVEAU, 1972–75
1⅛ x 5⅝ x 3⅛

Footnotes

[1]Dada, a movement that arose in Zurich during World War I (1914–1918) among young artists and writers, mostly exiles, who gave expression to what they perceived as the madness and chaos of the times. Their art, or rather, anti-art took the form of subject matter conventionally perceived as absurd. The term *Dada* may have meaning, specifically in French babytalk, "hobby-horse." Its purpose in this context is, however, to signify meaninglessness. Among the Dadaists were writers Hugo Ball, Richard Huelsenbeck, Rumanian poet Tristan Tzara, and artists Jean Arp and Marcel Janco.

[2]Marcel Duchamp (1887–1968), French painter. Duchamp redefined the concept of art by presenting ready-made, common objects as works of art, such as a bottle-drying rack, a urinal, and a bicycle wheel. The point is that artists themselves, not other authorities, whether religious, political, academic, etc., define what art is. His thinking was closely aligned with the Dadaists' iconoclastic ideas. When he went to New York in the 1920's, he and a handful of artists founded the Dada movement in America which proposed to liberate art from the confines of tradition. Duchamp is best remembered in the popular mind for his cubist-futurist canvas, *Nude Descending a Staircase,* the scandal of the New York Armory Show in 1913.

[3]Surrealism, an art movement founded by French poet and writer André Breton which replaced the weakening Dada in the first years after World War I but shared with it its nihilistic attitude toward academic institutions. Its adherents adopted the term "surréaliste" from the French poet and art critic Guillaume Appollinaire. To them it meant pure psychic automatism, when the subconscious mind of the artist gives expression to itself with unconventional and curious results. The surrealists were among the first to see the importance of the theories of Sigmund Freud for art.

[4]Paul Klee (1879–1940), a Swiss-born artist who moved to Munich in 1898 to study art. There, in 1912, he became associated with members of *Der Blaue Reiter* (The Blue Rider), an avant-garde group of German Expressionists. He taught at the Bauhaus and the Düsseldorf Academy. In 1925 he participated in the first Surrealist exhibition in Paris. When the Nazis labeled him a "degenerate artist," he returned to Switzerland. His art reflects the fantastical, personal form of art. He was interested in primitive art, art of children, and art of the insane.

[5]Kurt Schwitters (1887–1948), German artist. Early in his career Schwitters displayed the influence that cubism had on his art, but after 1919, his style was noticeably

affected by the Dada movement. He began to experiment with torn up throw-away objects in collages. In this way he approached the Dadaist notion of making art from non-art. He labeled his collages and "assemblages" as "Merz," a word that has no meaning.

[6]Max Ernst (1891–1976), German painter and sculptor. Ernst was first influenced by German Expressionism. After World War I he cofounded the irreverent Dada movement in Cologne, which opposed traditional art values. Soon after, he went to Paris where he played an important role in the development of Surrealism, an art which expresses the process of thought via psychic automatism. He escaped occupied Europe and came to the United States. Later he returned to Europe.

[7]Joseph Cornell (1903–1972), American sculptor noted for his boxes. Cornell started out as a painter and then began to experiment with "assemblages" of various objects in which he combined the sentimental with the bizarre, thus evoking memories and fantasies in this very personal form of expression.

[8]This conversation is a condensed and edited version of a series of taped interviews with Leo Rabkin, joined on the last day by Dorothy Rabkin, in his studio from June 10 to June 14, 1981, in New York.

[9]Gaston Bachelard, French philosopher, born 1884, studied chemistry and physics and became a college professor and natural scientist. Later he taught philosophy at the University of Dijon and the Collège de France. When Bachelard died in 1962 he was an honorary professor at the Sorbonne. His books, in addition to *The Poetics of Space,* include *The Experience of Space in Contemporary Physics, The Psychoanalysis of Fire, Water and Dreams, Air and Reverie, The Earth and the Reveries of the Will, The Earth and the Reveries of Rest,* among others.

[10]Rainer-Maria Rilke (1875–1926), Austrian born poet, noted for his use of symbols to communicate his inner world. In *Neue Gedichte* (1907) and *Die Neuen Gedichte* (1908), his masterpieces, he offered poems which expressed his idea of perfect form and movement in space conveying the presence of God. He was influenced by Impressionist painting and Symbolist poetry during a stay in Paris.

[11]Stéphane Mallarmé (1842–1898), French symbolist poet, was a chief influence on the new Symbolist school of the mid-1880's which originated in France as a reaction to the naturalism

and realism of the period. He maintained that the poet should express the ideas of a transcendental world. He saw parallels in the development of poetry and music, especially the music of Wagner. He taught English in lycées, wrote about fashion and through his *Poésies* and *Album de Vers et de Prose,* published in 1887, greatly affected the character of modern poetry.

[12]Shakers, a religious sect that originated in 1747 as an off-shoot of the Quakers in England. In 1776, some of its members emigrated to New York State and established a colony. They were a thrifty, hard-working and self-sustaining people, who made their own furniture, which was simple in design and solid in construction.

[13]Richard Lindner (1901–1978), German-born artist. Lindner left his native land in 1933. He lived for a time in Paris until 1941 when he moved to New York City. There he became successful as a commercial illustrator, but in the early 1950's he turned to painting. Lindner's art features large, smoothly modeled figures, interlocking forms and bright colors, frequently of women with sado-masochistic overtones. Lindner is regarded by critics as a proto-pop artist because of his deliberate satirizing of German and American "culture." He taught at the Pratt Institute in New York.

[14]Frank Stella (b. 1936), American painter. Stella emerged in the late 1950's when Abstract Expressionism had run its course. In contrast to the Abstract Expressionists' notion of art, he perceived an art-work as an object rather than as a reference to some extraneous matter or meaning. His concern was with the actual material of art. He was influenced by Jasper Johns in the idea of the relation of the image and the canvas. This led to his shaped painted canvases. His most recent large-scale works are three-dimensional paintings, garish in color and expressive in gesture and form.

[15]Yves Klein (1928–1962), French conceptual artist. Around 1960, in Nice he was grouped with the "New Realists," artists who strove to get away from the traditional idea of the easel picture. Seeing art as continual discovery, they laid emphasis on the reality of ideas, a reality beyond material and appearances. The activity of making an art-work becomes important; the finished work remains as an indication of the energy exerted in its creation. Klein's experiments with monochrome painting foreshadowed Minimal Art.

[16]Christo (Javacheff) (b. 1935), Bulgarian born artist living in New York, known for his packaging of objects or *empaquetages,* which may repre-

sent a comment on contemporary industrial society, its "product" culture, and its trend toward anonymity and nothingness. Christo is best known for monumental environmental works such as *Valley Curtain* (1971–1972) in Rifle, Colorado, and *Running Fence* (1976), a 24½-mile long construction of nylon fabric and steel cable and poles built in Sonoma and Marin Counties in California.

[17]Emil Nolde (1867–1956), German painter and graphic artist. Nolde associated for a short time with a group of German expressionists who called themselves *Die Brücke* (The Bridge) artists. Nolde used brilliant color in his paintings to communicate his intense emotions and ideas.

[18]Ad Reinhardt (1913–1967), American painter, was one of the earliest abstract artists in America. His credo of discipline and restraint was the antithesis of that which the contemporary action painters, such as Jackson Pollock, practiced. He was convinced that true art is the result of premedition and control, an idea that accorded with oriental art traditions. His final works, a series of monochrome black convases, reflect the oriental vein in his thinking as he sought to render the absolute by reducing signs of the artist's hand.

[19]Sol LeWitt (b. 1928), American artist. LeWitt's belief in the superior importance of idea over activity in the art creation process ties him to the conceptual artists. This belief manifests itself in his numerous drawings through which he documents with words and lines how his ideas find form. Throughout his career he has been preoccupied with the fundamental units of art, particularly the cube.

[20]George Grosz (1893–1959), German painter and graphic artist. During and after World War I he produced drawings that were biting comments on the corruption of society. His weapon was brutal realism intensified by caricature. He became active in a politically oriented German Dada movement. At this time he began executing political cartoons. The Nazis viewed him as an undesirable citizen because of his involvement in left-wing politics. He fled to the United States in 1933.

[21]The Bauhaus was a German school of architecture, design and craftsmanship that was founded at Weimar by Walter Gropius in 1919. Its program stressed the integration of various fields of the arts. In the face of the industrial age, it met with the challenge to connect art and industry more closely. Its teaching staff included

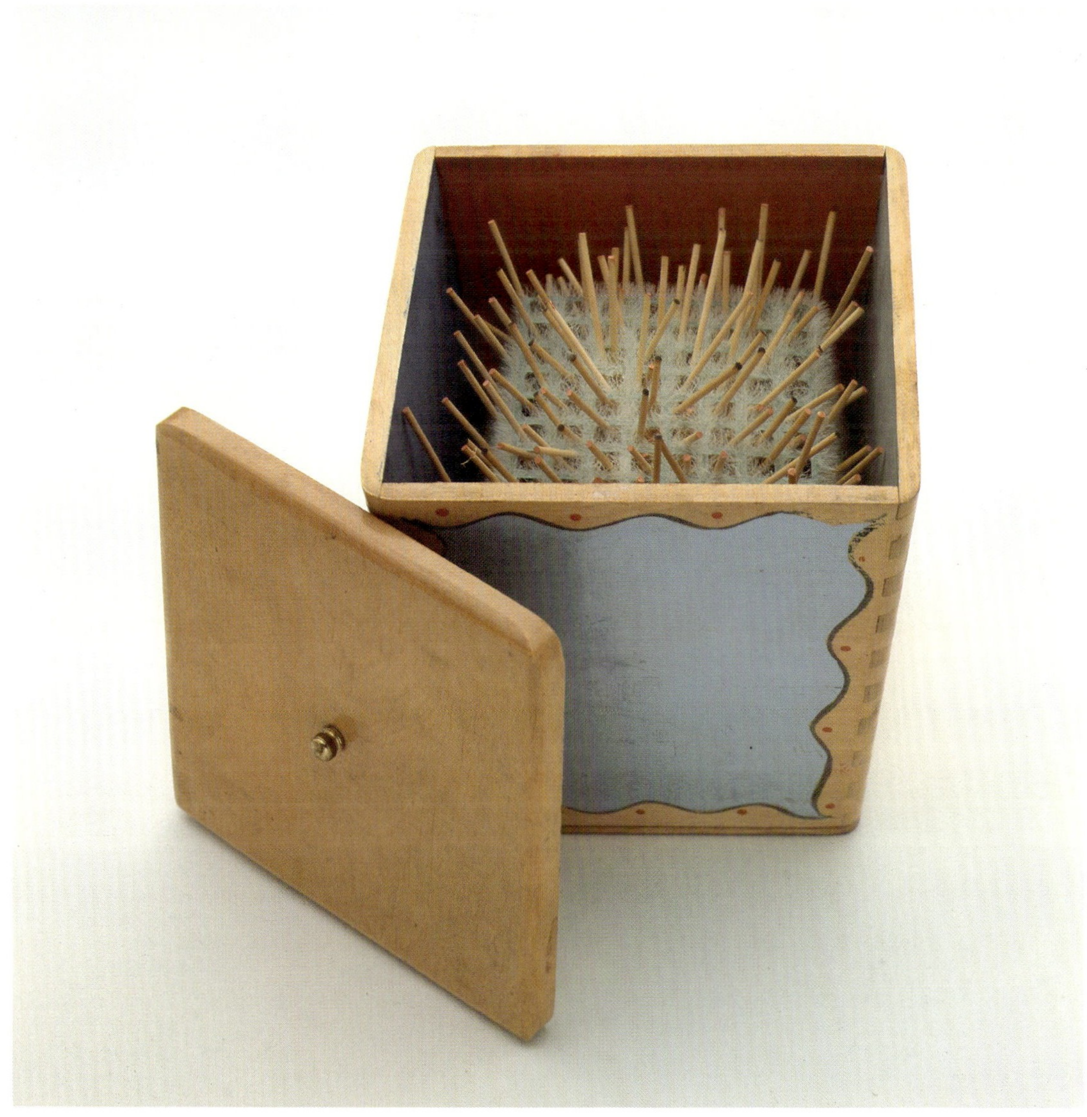

59 COMPUTERIZED KITCHEN, 1978
7 x 6 x 6

such masters as Lyonel Feininger, Vasili Kandinsky, and Paul Klee. It closed in 1933 due to Nazi hostility.

[22]American Abstract Artists was a group organized in 1936 when modern art in America was emerging as a strong force. Prior to this, in 1929, the Museum of Modern Art had been founded in New York. It was one of the first organizations ever to be devoted entirely to modern art. Many European artists fled to the United States at that time bringing with them theories of cubism and geometric abstraction. They provided a great source of inspiration for the group of American artists with whom they annually exhibited. The group exists today.

[23]Paul Cézanne (1839–1906), French painter. Cézanne came in contact with the Impressionists and recognized their contribution to the study of color and light. As they drew their subject matter directly from nature, so did he, but he eschewed their tendency to sacrifice form by rendering shapes in juxtapositions of tiny patches of color. Instead, Cézanne used color as a means of modeling. His compositions are highly organized, reminiscent of the classical tradition of the early 17th-century French painter Nicolas Poussin.

[24]Degenerate Art. In 1933 Hitler mounted a campaign to purge Germany of modern art. Under the Nazi regime, the general category of expressionist art was attacked as a corrupting influence. Artists, critics, dealers, etc., were forbidden to paint or exhibit. Many artists, like George Grosz, Oskar Kokoschka and Max Beckmann were forced to emigrate. Expressionist pictures were confiscated for an exhibition of Degenerate Art held in 1937 which was intended to arouse public disgust with its contents.

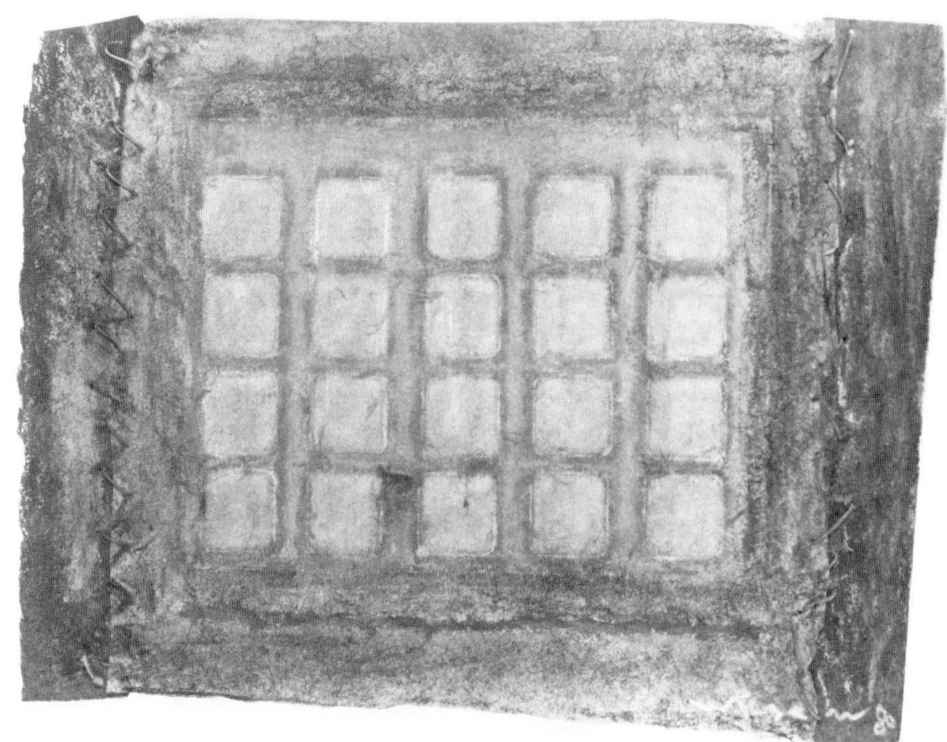

67 PASTEL—YELLOW WINDOWS, 1980
6 x 8

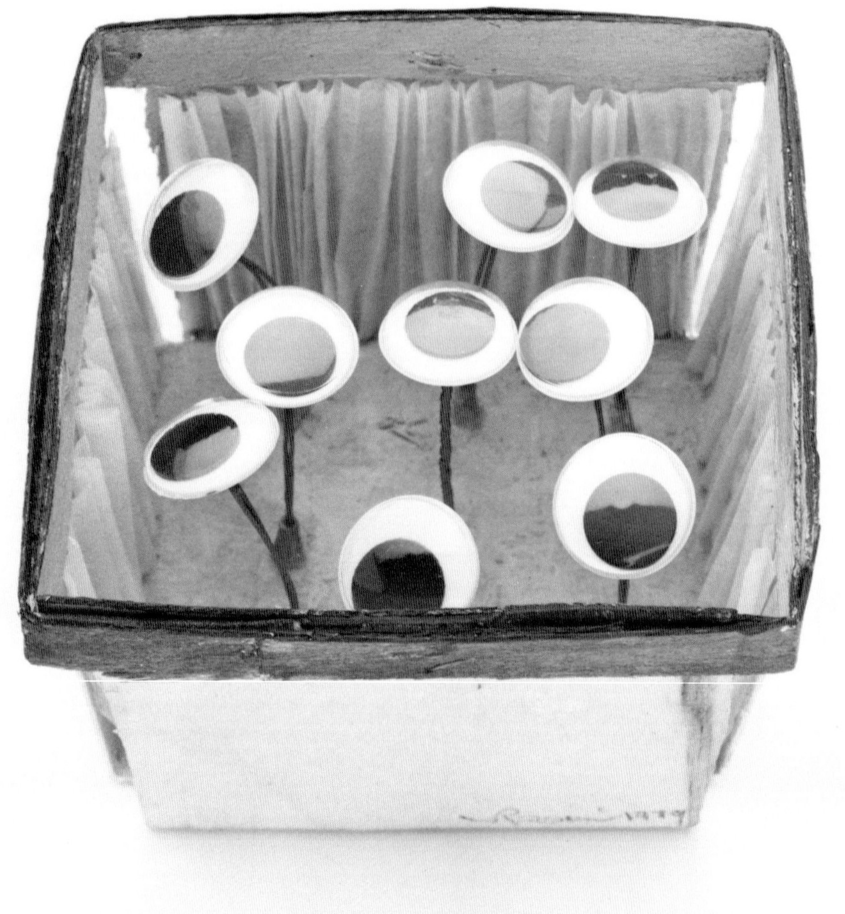

4-1 EIGHTEEN STRAWBERRY BOXES —
VARIATIONS ON A THEME
CHAMBRE À PLAISIR, 1960
2½ x 4¼ x 4¼

Catalogue List

1 ELEVEN PAINTED BUTTONS IN AN UNTANGLED WEB, 1959
Wood box. Outside: metallic paint. Top: wire springs and stenciling. Inside: acrylic paint, buttons, silk thread
1¼ x 5⅝ x 3⅛

2 JOY, BEAUTY, LIFE (TYRRELLS JBL CASCADE), 1959
Hinged wood box. Enamel paint on exterior sides. Inside top and bottom: folded paper, silk thread, paint
10⅛ x 5⅝ x 3½

3 CHARM BOX FOR WINTER, 1960
Hinged souvenir box (wood), outside-top and bottom: vinyl plastic findings (some stained). Inside cover: plastic findings, wood spheres, machined acrylic, acrylic paint. Bottom: prism, mirror, glass beads, plastic findings, monofilament
2½ x 6⅞ x 3¾

4 EIGHTEEN STRAWBERRY BOXES—VARIATIONS ON A THEME

1 CHAMBRE À PLAISIR, 1960
Pink acrylic paint, paper, mirrored beads, monofilament
2½ x 4¼ x 4¼

2 TWENTY NERVOUS TRIANGLES, 1960
Green acrylic paint, paper, mirrored beads, monofilament
2½ x 4¼ x 4¼

3 CAGE FOR THE TROPICS, 1971
Glass, plastic, wire screen, monofilament, tape
3 x 5⅜ x 5⅜

4 CATERING HALL, WEDDINGS, ETC., 1972
Enamel paint, convex mirror, translucent acrylic, aluminum foil, sequins, glass beads
2½ x 4¼ x 4¼

5 RESORT HOTEL, 1972
Enamel paint, faceted mirrors, monofilament, beads, sequins
2½ x 4¼ x 4¼

6 THE AUTOMOBILE, 1973–1979
Concave mirror, acrylic, enamel paint, tape, sequins, metal beads
2½ x 4¼ x 4¼

7 ADOBE FOR WEAVERS, 1979
Orange acrylic paint, folded translucent plastic, pencil
2½ x 4¼ x 4¼

8 BOX OF LOVE LETTERS, 1979
Folded tracing paper, beads, sequins, monofilament
2½ x 4¼ x 4¼

9 CAT'S CRADLE, 1979
Green acrylic paint, cotton string, white pencil, wire
2½ x 4¼ x 4¼

10 CHAPEL FOR POLITICAL PRAYERS, 1979
Acrylic paint, beads, translucent plastic, sequins
2½ x 4¼ x 4¼

11 CORPORATION CONFERENCE, 1979
Acrylic paint, red paper with pencil lines, beads, sequins, monofilament
2½ x 5⅜ x 3¾

12 HOUSE FOR THE OCEAN FLOOR, 1979
White acrylic paint, plastic, wire screening, glass, pebbles, acrylic
2½ x 3½ x 5⅜

13 MAUSOLEUM FOR GRAY GHOSTS, 1979
Aluminum paint, plastic, pencil lines, monofilament
2½ x 4¼ x 4¼

14 PAPER DOODLES, 1979
Orange acrylic paint, flocked and painted (watercolor) paper loops
1½ x 4 x 4

15 PAPER PALMS, 1979
Dark green acrylic paint, brass coils, wood beads, paper, cellophane, sequins
2½ x 5⅜ x 5⅜

16 PUBLIC CORRIDOR, 1979
Tracing paper, acrylic paint, sequins, beads, monofilament
2½ x 4¼ x 4¼

17 THIRTEEN UNSAFE SQUARES, 1979
Black and white paint, wood beads, brass coils, plastic toy parts
3 x 5⅜ x 5⅜

18 WORLD TRADE CENTER I AND II, 1979
Acrylic paint, translucent acrylic, aluminum foil, sequins, glass beads, monofilament
2½ x 4¼ x 4¼

5 THE HABITAT OF THE HERMIT CRAB, 1960
Hinged lacquered oriental wood box. Cover-inside: machined acrylic. Bottom: folded paper, glass beads, monofilament, machined acrylic
2⅛ x 10 x 3⅝

6 SPARKLERS AND MOON, 1960
Wood box. Cover-top: enamel paint with metal buttons (costume jewelry findings). Bottom-inside: mother-of-pearl buttons, glass beads, monofilament, box lined with machined acrylic. Machined acrylic disc glued to bottom (outside)
1⅜ x 5⅝ x 3⅛

7 NERVOUS BOX, 1961
Wood box. Outside: enamel paint with stenciling on cover. Inside-bottom: plastic ball-point pen parts, beads, machined acrylic, monofilament
1⅛ x 5⅝ x 3⅛

8 CREATIVE, IMITATIVE, 1963
Cover-outside: stapled ribbon & tape. Inside: staples projecting from outside. Bottom-outside: plastic (vinyl), rhinestones, acrylic paint. Inside: pine cone scales, glass beads, monofilament, acrylic paint
1½ x 11⅛ x 5

9 INTUITION, PREMONITION AND SUSPICION, 1963
Wood box. Outside: enamel paint with metal and plastic findings on cover. Inside cover: acrylic paint. Bottom: glass beads, plastic (vinyl and machined acrylic), monofilament
1½ x 5⅝ x 3⅛

10 RAIN BOX, 1963
Unpainted wooden box with sliding cover. Inside: Convex mirrors, wood and glass beads, machined acrylic, monofilament
2½ x 14¾ x 4¾

11 CRYSTAL BEADS, 1964
Plastic box (machined acrylic). Inside: crystal faceted cubes (beads). Mirrored base, single cube (plastic) on or nearby.
7 x 6⅞ x 6⅞

12 FORMAL PAPER GARDEN, 1964
Formed paper, watercolor, pastel, and flocking
4¼ x 6⅝

13 GOOSE STEP BOX, 1964
Wood box. Cover-outside: painted lace. Inside: unpainted. Bottom-inside: wood clothes pins, metal screws, springs, machine acrylic
1¼ x 5¾ x 3¼

14 GREEN GLASS-WHITE BEADS, 1964
Plastic box (machine acrylic). Inside: glass beads, acrylic sheets, monofilament. Two parts. Mirror
7⅝ cube

15 SILVER JELLO, 1964
Hinged wood cigar box. Cover top: cotton embroidered binding, enamel paint. Inside: enamel paint. Bottom-outside: enamel paint. Inside: convex mirrors, machined acrylic, plastic tape, monofilament
3 x 10¼ x 6¾

16 DRAWING FOR A TENT FLOOR, 1966
Ink on acrylic, plastic sphere and disk
6 x 4¼ x 2½

17 CAGE FOR SEEDS AND BEADS, 1967
Plastic box (machined acrylic). Inside: New Jersey goat's beard seed, wood beads, wood sticks, string, machined acrylic
7⅛ x 6 x 6

18 DRAWING FOR A TENT FLOOR, 1967
Ink on acrylic, plastic sphere and disk
6 x 4¼ x 2½

19 GROWN IN MECCA CALIFORNIA, 1968
Wood date fruit box. Bottom-inside: corset stays, monofilament
1¾ x 14 x 5¾

20 INDIAN BEAD BOX, 1969
Plastic box (machined acrylic). Inside: strung antique American Indian beads, monofilament
12 x 10⅛ x 10⅛

21 MONASTIC CELLS, 1969
Wood box with machined acrylic sliding cover. Inside: mica, sticks (wood), machined acrylic, acrylic paint
1⅝ x 8¾ x 4⅛

22 PORCH, 1969
Wood box. Cover-outside and inside: inscribed foil. Bottom inside: mirror, buttons, toothpicks, colored threads
1⅛ x 5¾ x 3¼

23 CORRAL WITH SUNSET, 1970
Wood box. Cover-outside: plastic "tesserae," enamel paint. Bottom-inside: glass and wood beads, wood sticks and spheres
1¼ x 5¾ x 3¼

24 DOUBLE CURTAIN BOX, 1970
Plastic box (machined acrylic), removable sides of translucent machined acrylic. Inside: plastic and glass beads, monofilament
5⅝ x 8⅜ x 4¾

25 HOTEL SUITE DELUXE, 1970
Plastic Box (machined acrylic). Inside: plastic jewelry findings, plastic and glass beads, mother of pearl buttons, monofilament
9⅛ x 7¼ x 7¼

26 HOUSE OF PAPER DOODLES, 1970
Plastic box (machined acrylic). Inside: machined acrylic, formed paper, glass beads, monofilament
6⅑ x 7¼ x 7¼

27 STAMPED AND CREASED (ORANGE FLOCKED LINE), 1970
Stamped watercolor with flocking
7¾ x 6⅝

28 CANNED RINGS, 1971
Plastic box (machined acrylic). Inside: vinyl loops, glass beads, monofilament
7 x 6 x 6

29 DISTORTED PAPER THRESHOLD IN MOTHER'S HOUSE, 1971
Hinged wood box from vanity or dresser. Inside-top and bottom: cut paper, mirrors
3⅛ x 8¾ x 6¼

30 FOLDED, STITCHED, AND FLOCKED—FOLKTALE FOR A SIMPLE CULTURE, 1971
Watercolor and tracing paper, thread, flocking on acrylic sheets
7 x ½ x 6 x ⅝

31 HOW TO WRAP NINETEEN-AND-A-HALF SCROLLS, 1971
Oriental and tracing papers, ink, watercolor, string and flocking on acrylic sheets
5⅜ x 5⅝ x ⅝

32 ORIENTAL LACQUER BOX OF BIRD BUILDING A NEST, 1971
Wood Japanese souvenir box. Cover-top: original lacquer and paint. Inside: painted (acrylic) wood sticks, string, wood beads
1½ x 9⅝ x 3¼

33 SIXTY-SIX LOOPS IN THE SUNSET, 1971
Oriental and tracing papers, ink and watercolor on acrylic sheets
7⅛ x 7⅛ x ⅝

34 KINDERGARTEN ART NOUVEAU, 1972–75
Wood box. Outside: enamel paint with rhinestones on cover (top). Inside: acrylic paint, paper loops (stamped and/or flocked), metal tacks
1⅛ x 5⅝ x 3⅛

35 FOLIES BERGÈRE, 1972
Wood box with machined acrylic cover (including metal handle). Bottom-inside: sea seeds, machine acrylic, acrylic paint, mylar, monofilament
4 x 7⅞ x 4⅝

36 NEW JERSEY GOAT'S BEARD (TRAGOPOGON PRATENSIS), 1972
Wood box with machined acrylic both cover and bottom. Inside: goat's beard weed
3 x 4⅞ x 4⅝

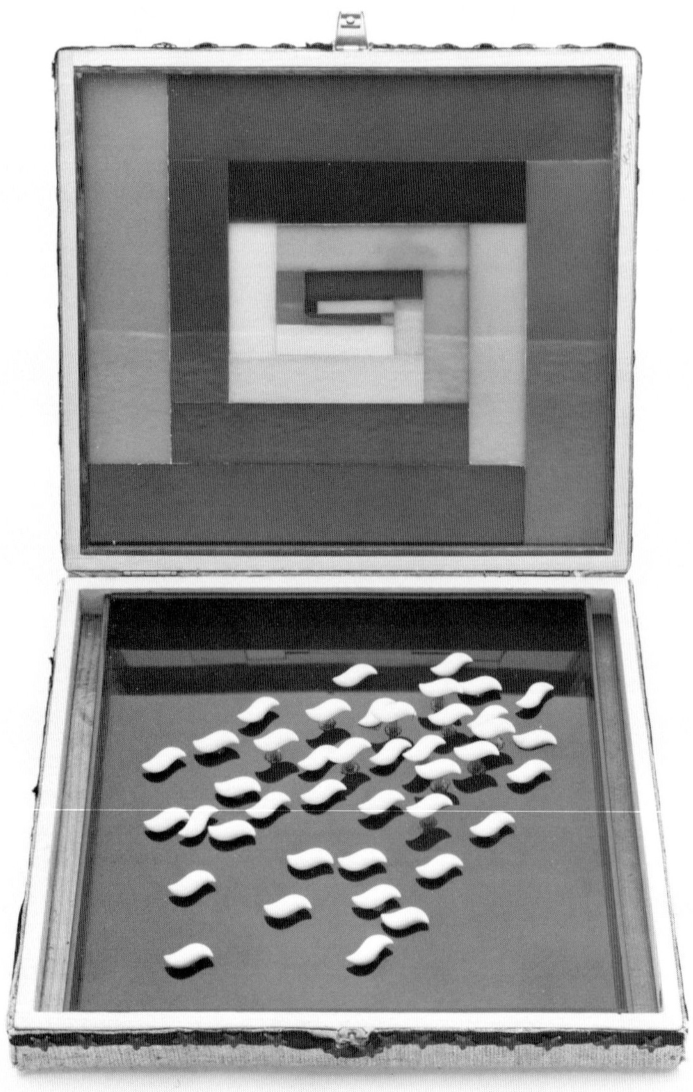

44 FLIGHT OF THE COMMAS, 1975
1¾ x 10½ x 9½

37 POINT CENTER, 1972
Plastic box (machined acrylic). Four parts taped together. Inside surface sandblasted and painted with acrylic paint, stamped
10 cube

38 TOSSED THOUGHTS IN A CARIBBEAN VILLA, 1973
Wood box with machined acrylic cover. Outside-bottom: oilcloth, cotton stitching. Inside-bottom: glass and plastic beads, metal findings, machined acrylic, acrylic paint, monofilament
3½ x 5 x 4⅝

39 BALLROOM, 1973
Hinged wood box from vanity or dresser with original paint on cover. Cover-inside: mirror. Bottom-inside: machined acrylic, plastic spheres (pharmaceutical, for deodorant dispensing), mirror
3¼ x 10¾ x 6½

40 CONSERVATORY, 1973
Plastic box (machined acrylic). Inside: plastic jewelry findings, plastic and glass beads, monofilament
6 x 7⅛ x 7⅛

41 PLAYHOUSE 5629, 1973
Hinged wood slide box for lectures. Inside-top: machined acrylic. Bottom: Plastic spheres (acrylic), paper loops, glass beads, monofilament, acrylic paint
4½ x 5½ x 5¼

42 COMFORTABLE HOUSEHOLD, 1974
Unpainted round wooden box. Inside-bottom: flocked plastic loops, concave mirror, mylar
2½ x 6 diameter

43 GARAGE—ROOF LEVEL, 1974
Watercolor, collage
7¼ x 7¼

44 FLIGHT OF THE COMMAS, 1975
Hinged wood candy box (German). Outside: covered with linen, ribbon, metal tacks (star-shaped). Inside-top: machined acrylic. Bottom: plastic findings, machined acrylic
1¾ x 10½ x 9½

45 FORMED PAPER—CIRCLES, 1975
Collage with pastel over formed paper
14 x 11

46 SHOCK BOX, 1975
Wood candy box (German). Outside covered with oilcloth. Bottom-inside: painted wood sticks, copper wire
1¾ x 11⅛ x 5

47 TWO HUNDRED TWENTY-FOUR 'D'S WITH ONE 'C', 1975
Plastic box (machined acrylic) with glass hospital beads, monofilament
9⅝ x 8⅛ x 8⅛

48 AQUARIUM, 1976
Wood candy box (German). Outside-top: painted lines on plastic tape. Sides: cotton embroidered trimming (border). Inside-top: machined acrylic, tape. Bottom: paintbrush handles (wood), rhinestones, acrylic paint
1⅝ x 10½ x 9¼

49 HOUSE OF WHITE LEAVES, 1976
Wooden part of barbershop appliance (box). Outside-top: wood and glass beads, ink drawing over contact paper. Sides: contact paper. Front: machined acrylic, wood beads, wire, string. Inside: name tags with string, monofilament, acrylic paint
9⅞ x 14 x 10¾

50 RED DOTS & STRING SQUARES, 1976
Formed paper, watercolor, and black thread stitching. Pastel
7¼ x 7¼

51 TWENTY MAN-MADE MOUNTAINS, 1976
Collage, watercolor, and cut paper
6½ x 6¼

52 WIRE GRID BOX, 1976
Plastic box (machined acrylic) with steel wire. Two parts. Mirror
8 cube

53 AMETHYST, 1977
Hinged wood candy box (German). Top-outside: wood strips. Inside: acrylic paint. Bottom-inside: glass costume jewelry and metal findings, wood, acrylic paint
9¼ x 10½ x 1½

54 CALABASH, 1977
Hinged souvenir lacquered wood box. Inside-top and bottom: molded rag paper, wood sticks, yarn, Guatemalan cloth, acrylic paint
3⅛ x 10 x 3¾

55 DOCUMENTS FOR A WELL-TEMPERED CODE, 1977
Hinged souvenir wood box. Machined acrylic, assorted plastic, wood sticks, plastic tape, acrylic paint
3¾ x 9 x 6½

56 FLIGHT OF THE GEESE, 1977
Collage and watercolor
6 x 6

57 STRATEGY—IMPASS OF THE RED & WHITE, 1977
Collage with loops, stamping, watercolor and tempera
10⅜ x 9⅞ framed

58 CHINESE HALF BOX, 1978
(Seven parts—A–F (watercolor box is G). Half-round wood box and watercolors on Thai paper
Box: diameter 8⅝ x 5⅝ x 1⅜
Watercolors: 10¼ x 7¼

59 COMPUTERIZED KITCHEN, 1978
Wood food canister. Outside-top: metal knob. Bottom: enamel paint on one side. Inside-bottom: flocked plastic fruit container, wood sticks, acrylic and enamel paint
7 x 6 x 6

60 CREASED WITH RED, 1978
Watercolor with flocking
8¾ x 5½

61 DUKE OF ORMOND, 1978
Hinged wood cigar box. Sides: acrylic paint. Cover: stenciled acrylic and metallic paint. Inside: plastic disks (eyes), wood dowels, acrylic paint
2¾ x 8¾ x 5⅝

62 NUMBER ONE, 1978
Watercolor (creased), string and beads
34⅝ x 34⅝

63 ARCHIVES FOR OLD LAW TENEMENTS, 1979
Hinged wood box. Outside: assorted wood trimmings and metal tacks. Inside-top and bottom: lined with contact paper. Bottom: folded oriental (Japanese, Thai, Chinese) paper, watercolor, monofilament
6 x 11½ x 7¼

64 ROPE PASTEL IN RED, 1979
Formed paper, pastel
17¼ x 16⅞ framed

65 ART 345, FRISCHE EIER, 1980
Wood candy box (German). Cover-top: wood, machined acrylic, tape, clothespin parts. Bottom-inside: formed paper, wire, beads, monofilament, acrylic paint
2¾ x 8⅛ x 3¾

66 CHAMBER OF ARCHAELOGICAL FRETWORK, 1980
Hinged wood cigar box. Outside-top and bottom: translucent machined acrylic over tape, tacks, beads. Inside: scallop shells, beads, ink, aluminum paint, monofilament
1¾ x 9½ x 7¼

67 PASTEL—YELLOW WINDOWS, 1980
Formed paper, pastel and string
6 x 8

68 SECONDARIES, 1980
Pleated oriental paper, string, and wood beads
18 x 18 plus string

69 UNTITLED, 1980
Watercolor (creased), string, and beads
19 x 19

70 AAA—5 STAR, 1981
Hinged wood cigar box. Entire box with gesso and egg tempera. Bottom-inside: folded tracing paper, machined acrylic in addition to the above
1¾ x 9¼ x 6½

71 BANJO NOTATIONS, 1981
Hinged wood candy box (German). Cover-outside: metallic rickrack trimming, acrylic paint. Inside: machined acrylic, acrylic paint. Inside-bottom: machined acrylic, acrylic paint
1⅝ x 10⅜ x 9⅜

72 MORNING, NOON AND AFTER, 1981
Wood box for shipping dry fruit. Outside-top: contact paper, metal handle, wood hinge, wire, tacks. Bottom: copper findings, wire, tacks. Inside-cover: copper and steel wire. Bottom: machined acrylic, lacquer and acrylic paint, plastic findings
2¼ x 7½ x 11¼

73 MUSIC HALL, 1981
Sealed wooden box with wooden spools, machined acrylic, special optical acrylic (3-M), metal bells
12 x 13¼ x 10¼

74 ORANGE STRING, 1981
Watercolor, string, and beads
25 x 25
Collection of Mrs. Sidamon-Eristoff, New York

75 PAPER WALNUT SHELLS WITH NET, 1981
Hinged wood box from vanity or dresser. Outside-top paint (enamel) metal star-shaped tack. Inside-cover: mirror, acrylic paint. Bottom: formed paper painted with acrylic paint, mirror, beads, monofilament
3 x 8¾ x 6

76 PARA TABACOS TORCIDOS, 1981
Hinged wood cigar box with gesso. Top-outside: original label with tempera paint. Inside: tempera paint. Bottom-inside: folded translucent plastic, acrylic paint, thumbtacks
1 x 7⅛ x 7½

77 PERU, 1981
Pleated oriental paper, string and wood beads
25 x 25 plus string

78 PURPLE DIVIDING RED & GREEN, 1981
Watercolor (creased), string and beads
25 x 25

79 RED LINE, 1981
Watercolor (creased), string and beads
25 x 25

80 ROPE PASTEL IN PURPLE AND GREEN, 1981
Formed paper, pastel
10½ x 12½

81 RUNNELS, THOUGHTS VEERING, 1981
Hinged wood cigar box. Outside-top and bottom: enamel paint with stenciling. Inside-top: wood spheres, painted (enamel) and unpainted, acrylic paint. Bottom: cork cylinders, stamped metal (copper), styrofoam, acrylic paint
3½ x 10 x 9

82 UNTITLED, 1981
Watercolor (creased), string and beads
25 x 25

83 VALE OF TEARS, 1981
Hinged cigar box covered with oil cloth, star-shaped metal tacks, cotton stitching on top, enamel paint on bottom. Cover-inside: marbelized paper, staples. Bottom-inside: formed and machined acrylic, paper loops (watercolor and flocked)
2½ x 6½ x 7⅜

84 VERY SIMPLE MOTION GRANTED, 1981
Hinged wood candy box (German). Top-outside: wood veneer (from tobacco packaging). Inside: aluminum and acrylic paint. Bottom-inside: machined acrylic and assorted plastic, copper wire
1¾ x 10¾ x 9½

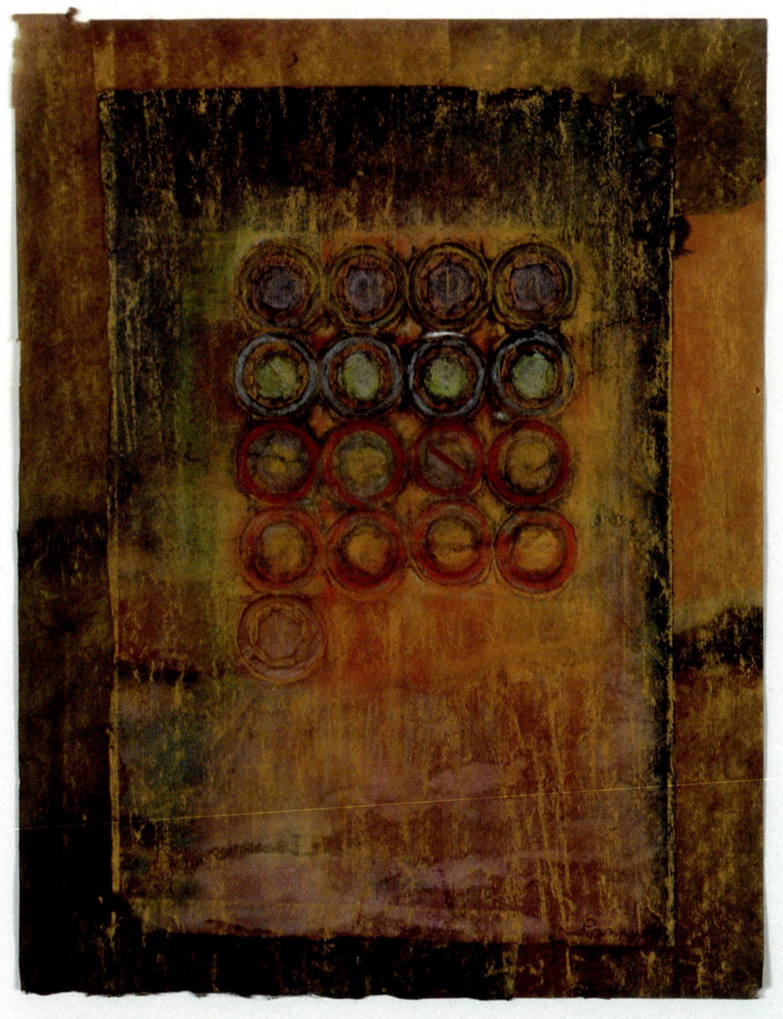

45 FORMED PAPER—CIRCLES, 1975
14 x 11

Exhibitions

Solo

Stairway Gallery, New York, New York, September 6–September 24, 1954.

Latow Gallery, New York, New York, April 4–May 6, 1961.

Louis Alexander Gallery, New York, New York, November 27–December 15, 1962.

Louis Alexander Gallery, New York, New York, March 27–April 14, 1963.

Richard Feigen Gallery, New York, New York, April 27–May 22, 1965.

Gertrude Kasle Gallery, Detroit, Michigan, September 19–October 15, 1965.

Richard Feigen Gallery, New York, New York, Beginning June 24, 1967.

Storm King Art Center, Mountainville, New York, *Leo Rabkin: Paintings and Shadow Boxes as Sculptural Images,* May 3–July 12, 1970. Catalogue with essay by Una E. Johnson.

Benson Gallery, Bridgehampton, New York, 1970.

Fairleigh Dickenson University, Madison, New Jersey, *From In My Studio Construction—For Private Viewing,* September 27–October 29, 1971.

Allentown Art Museum, Allentown, Pennsylvania, *Leo Rabkin,* October 2–November 20, 1977. Catalogue with essay by Susan C. Larsen.

Truman Gallery, New York, New York, *Boxes,* March 24–April 15, 1978.

Truman Gallery, New York, New York, *Strawberry Boxes and Watercolors,* February 1–April 25, 1979.

Parsons-Dreyfuss Gallery, New York, New York, April 1–April 19, 1980.

Hal Bromm Gallery, New York, New York, September 6–September 30, 1980.

Marilyn Pearl Gallery, New York, New York, October 10–November 5, 1981.

Massimo Minini, Milan, Italy, 1981.

La Jolla Museum of Contemporary Art, La Jolla, California, *Leo Rabkin Works,* October 3–November 15, 1981. Catalogue with essay and interview by Robert McDonald.

Group

Laurel Gallery, New York, New York, *New York University Group Show,* April 10–April 20, 1950.

Addison Gallery of American Art, Phillips Academy, Andover, Massachusetts, *Art Schools U.S.A.: Third Annual Exhibition,* 1951.

March Gallery, New York, New York, *Tenth Street Cooperative, January 8*–January 28, 1959.

Hirschl and Adler Gallery, New York, New York, *Experiences in Art I,* November 11–December 28, 1959. Catalogue.

Hirschl and Adler Gallery, New York, New York, *Experiences in Art II,* December 8–December 31, 1959. Catalogue.

The Brooklyn Museum, Brooklyn, New York, *Brooklyn Museum Watercolor Exhibition,* 1959.

Whitney Museum of American Art, New York, New York, *1959 Paintings Annual,* December 9, 1959–January 8, 1960. Catalogue.

Martha Jackson Gallery, New York, New York, *New Form—New Media I,* June 6–June 24, 1960. Catalogue.

Signa Gallery, East Hampton, New York, *Open Group Show,* June 24–July 21, 1960.

Museum of Modern Art, New York, New York, *New Talents,* September 20–October 30, 1960.

Martha Jackson Gallery, New York, New York, *New Form—New Media II,* September 27–October 22, 1960.

Washington Square Gallery, New York, New York, *Group Show,* October 26–November 27, 1960.

Whitney Museum of American Art, New York, New York, *Annual of Sculpture and Drawings,* December 6, 1960–January 22, 1961. Catalogue.

Tirca Karlis Gallery, Provincetown, Massachusetts, *Group Show,* 1960.

Silvermine Guild: Center for the Arts, New Canaan, Connecticut, *Twelfth New England Exhibition,* June 18–July 16, 1961. Catalogue.

Whitney Museum of American Art, New York, New York, *Annual Exhibition of Contemporary Painting,* December 13, 1961–February 4, 1962. Catalogue.

The Museum of Modern Art, New York, New York, *Recent Acquisitions,* December 19, 1961–February 25, 1962.

Carneal House, Covington, Kentucky, *Two Man Show,* 1961.

Solomon R. Guggenheim Museum, New York, New York, *Summer Selections, 1962,* July 3–September 30, 1962.

Workshop Gallery, New York, New York, *Group Show,* November 1–November 21, 1962.

Louis Alexander Gallery, New York, New York, *A Holiday Exhibition,* December 18, 1962–January 5, 1963.

American Federation of Arts, New York, New York, *Affinities,* November 5–November 26, 1962, Ohio University, Athens, Ohio; December 11, 1962–January 3, 1963, Brooks Memorial Art Gallery, Memphis, Tennessee; February 14–March 14, 1963, Milwaukee Art Center, Milwaukee, Wisconsin; March 28–April 18, 1963, Frye Art Museum, Seattle, Washington; May 5–May 26, 1963, Montclair Art Museum, Montclair, New Jersey; July 9–July 23, 1963, Adelphi College, Garden City, Long Island, New York; August 1–October 6, 1963, Tennessee Fine Arts Center, Nashville, Tennessee.

Silvermine Guild: Center for the Arts, New Canaan, Connecticut, *14th Annual: New England Artists,* June 23–July 9, 1963.

Betty Parsons Gallery, New York, New York, *Toys by Artists,* Beginning December, 1963.

Museo del Arte Moderna, Genoa, Italy, *Watercolor,* 1963.

East Hampton Gallery, New York, New York, *American Abstract Artists,* 1963.

Traveling Exhibitions, The Museum of Modern Art, New York, New York, *Abstract Watercolors by 14 Americans,* organized by (but not exhibited at) the International Council of the Museum of Modern Art and circulated to 7 institutes throughout the United States and to Yugoslavia, Greece, India, Ceylon, Australia and New Zealand, 1963. Catalogue.

Silvermine Guild: Center for the Arts, New Canaan, Connecticut, *15th Annual New England Exhibition,* June 21–July 16, 1964.

Franklin Siden Gallery, Detroit, Michigan, *Group Show,* Beginning July, 1964.

Whitney Museum of American Art, New York, New York, *1964 Sculpture Annual,* December 9, 1964–January 31, 1965. Catalogue.

Traveling Exhibition, American Federation of Arts, New York, New York, *Two Year Loan Exhibit,* organized by (but not exhibited at) American Federation of Arts and circulated to the American Embassy at Copenhagen, Denmark, 1964.

Byron Gallery, New York, New York, *100 American Drawings,* 1964.

Byron Gallery, New York, New York, *Boxes,* 1964.

Ciba-Geigy Corporation, Ardsley, New York, *Art Exhibit,* 1964.

Cranbrook Academy of Art Museum, Bloomfield Hills, Michigan, *Paintings and Sculpture from the University of Michigan Collection,* January 1–January 31, 1965.

University of Michigan Museum of Art, Ann Arbor, Michigan, *One Hundred Contemporary American Drawings,* February 24–March 28, 1965. Catalogue.

Staatliche Kunsthalle, Baden-Baden, West Germany, *10 Jahresausstellung Malerei und Plastik,* June 4–July 5, 1965. Catalogue.

Museum of Modern Art, New York, New York, *Editions in Art,* June 23–August 1, 1965.

Solomon R. Guggenheim Museum, New York, New York, *Some Recent Gifts,* July 20–August 29, 1965.

Museum of Art, Rhode Island School of Design, Providence, Rhode Island, *Contemporary Boxes and Wall Sculpture,* September 23–October 17, 1965. Catalogue.

Loeb Student Center, New York University, New York, New York, *New York University Art Alumni Exhibition,* October 11–October 22, 1965. Catalogue.

Whitney Museum of American Art, New York, New York, *1965 Painting Annual,* December 8, 1965–January 30, 1966. Catalogue.

Riverside Museum, New York, New York, *American Abstract Artists,* 1965.

Gallery of Modern Art, New York, New York, *Drawing Society Exhibit,* 1965.

Manhattanville College, New York, New York, *College Teachers Collection,* 1965.

Graham Gallery, New York, New York, *Artists for Core,* 1965.

Gertrude Kasle Gallery, Detroit, Michigan, *Trio of Water-colorists,* 1965.

Finch College Museum of Art, New York, New York, *Recent Acquisitions,* 1965.

Stedelijk Van Abbe-Museum, Eindhoven, Netherlands, *Kunst-Licht-Kunst,* September 25–December 4, 1966. Catalogue with statements of the artists.

Aldrich Museum of Contemporary Art, Ridgefield, Connecticut, *The John G. Powers Collection,* September 25–December 11, 1966. Catalogue.

Whitney Museum of American Art, New York, New York, *1966 Annual of Sculpture and Prints,* December 16, 1966–February 5, 1967. Catalogue.

Flint Institute of Art, Dewaters Art Center, Flint, Michigan, *Group Show,* 1966.

Rabkin's Studio, New York, New York, *Kineticism,* Historical Exhibition and Lecture by Willoughby Sharp, 1966.

College Art Gallery, Drew University, Madison, New Jersey, *Two Man Show,* 1966.

Galerie Eleana Sonnabend, Paris, France, *Art Electric,* 1966.

Riverside Museum, New York, New York, *Thirteenth Anniversary Exhibition of the American Abstract Artists,* 1966.

Flint Institute of Art, Dewaters Art Center, Flint, Michigan, *Five Detroit Galleries,* 1966.

Betty Parsons Gallery, New York, New York, *Sculpture,* 1966.

Howard Wise Gallery, New York, New York, *Lights in Orbit,* February 4–March 4, 1967.

Walker Art Center, Minneapolis, Minnesota, *Light, Motion, Space,* April 8–June 24, 1967; Milwaukee Art Center, Milwaukee, Wisconsin, June 24–July 30, 1967. Catalogue.

Ciba-Geigy Corporation, Ardsley, New York, *Art Exhibit,* April 22–May 6, 1967. Catalogue.

New Jersey State Museum, Trenton, New Jersey, *Focus on Light,* May 20–September 10, 1967. Catalogue.

George Washington Hotel, New York, New York, *Luminism,* One-Night Exhibition arranged for the Artist's Club by Willoughby Sharp and Kineticism Press, May 25, 1967. Catalogue.

New York State Fair Expo, Syracuse, New York, *Art Today 1967,* August 29–September 4, 1967.

Traveling Exhibitions, The Smithsonian Institute, Washington, D.C., *New Expressions in Fine Printmaking,* organized by (but not exhibited at) the Smithsonian Institute and circulated through Germany, Belgium, France, Switzerland and Yugoslavia, September 15, 1967–September 15, 1970. Catalogue.

Galerie Eleana Sonnabend, Paris, France, *Art Electric,* 1967.

Henry Gallery, Washington, D.C., *Group Show,* 1967.

Riverside Museum, New York, New York, *Federation of Modern Painters and Sculptors: 27 Annual Exhibition,* January 14–February 19, 1968.

University Art Museum, University of California, Berkeley, California, *Selections 1968,* August 6–September 15, 1968. Catalogue.

American Craft Museum, New York, New York, *Plastic as Plastic,* September 23, 1968–January 12, 1969. Catalogue.

Whitney Museum of American Art, New York, New York, *1968 Annual Exhibition of Sculpture,* December 17, 1968–January 19, 1969. Catalogue.

The Brooklyn Museum, New York, New York, *16th National Print Exhibition—Two Decades of American Prints, 1947–68,* 1968.

Finch College Museum of Art, New York, New York, *Destruction Art—Destroy to Create,* 1968.

Finch College Museum of Art, New York, New York, *Betty Parsons' Private Collection,* 1968.

North Carolina Museum of Art, Raleigh, North Carolina, *American Abstract Artists,* February 9–March 9, 1969. Catalogue.

West Chester Art Society, West Chester, Pennsylvania, Organized by Ciba-Geigy Corporation, *Business Collects Art: The Geigy Collection,* November 12–December 3, 1969.

Jewish Museum, New York, New York, *Plastic Presence,* November 14, 1969–January 4, 1970; Milwaukee Art Center, Milwaukee, Wisconsin, January 30–March 8, 1970; San Francisco Museum of Art, San Francisco, California, April 24–May 24, 1970. Catalogue.

Sculptor's Guild Gallery, New York, New York, *Some New Members,* November 28–October 30, 1969.

The Society of the Four Arts, Palm Beach, Florida, *31st Annual Exhibition of Contemporary American Painting,* December 6–December 28, 1969.

Whitney Museum of American Art, New York, New York, *1969 Annual Exhibition of Painting,* December 16, 1969–February 1, 1970. Catalogue.

Smithsonian Museum, Washington, D.C., *Plastic as Plastic,* Organized by (but not exhibited at) American Craft Museum, New York, New York, 1969.

Martha Jackson, New York, New York, *Chase Manhattan Bank Collection,* January 26–January 31, 1970.

The Brooklyn Museum, Brooklyn, New York, *17th Annual Print Exhibition,* June 1–September 1, 1970. Catalogue.

Aldrich Museum of Contemporary Art, Ridgefield, Connecticut, *Acquisitions for the Museum of Modern Art, 1959 Through 1969,* September 27, 1970–January 3, 1971.

Lever House, New York, New York, *Group Show,* Organized by (but not exhibited at) Sculptor's Guild, New York, New York, 1970.

Loeb Center, New York University, New York, New York, *American Abstract Artists,* 1970.

The Society of the Four Arts, Palm Beach, Florida, *32nd Annual Exhibit of Contemporary Painting,* 1970.

Randolph-Macon College, Lynchburg, Virginia, *Group Show,* 1970.

Bayonne Public Library, Bayonne, New Jersey, *Geigy Chemical Corporation Art Collection,* 1970.

Honolulu Academy of Arts, *First Hawaii National Print Exhibition,* February 4–March 7, 1971. Catalogue.

Hudson River Museum, Yonkers, New York, *A New Consciousness: The Ciba-Geigy Collection,* February 6–March 7, 1971.

Members Gallery, Albright-Knox Art Gallery, Buffalo, New York, *Sculpture and Graphics,* Beginning April 1, 1971.

Lever House, New York, New York, *Group Show,* Organized by (but not exhibited at) Sculptor's Guild, New York, New York, October 30–November 21, 1971.

Louisville Free Public Library, Louisville, Kentucky, *Plastic Possibilities,* 1971.

American Academy and Institute of Arts and Letters, New York, New York, *Contemporary Painting and Sculpture,* March 3–April 9, 1972.

Brooklyn Museum, Brooklyn, New York, *18th National Print Exhibition,* November 22, 1972–February 4, 1973; Palace of the Legion of Honor, San Francisco, California, March 24–June 17, 1973. Catalogue.

Federation of Modern Painters and Sculptors, Union Carbide Exhibition Hall, New York, New York, *Group Show,* March 15–March 30, 1973.

Whitney Museum of American Art, New York, New York, *Tribute to John I. H. Bauer,* June 5–June 25, 1974.

Lever House, New York, New York, *Group Show,* Organized by (but not exhibited at) Sculptor's Guild, New York, New York, October 27–November 17, 1974. Catalogue.

Landmark Gallery, New York, New York, *118 Artists' Drawings,* December 21, 1974–January 9, 1975.

Whitney Museum of American Art, New York, New York, *20th Century Drawings from the Permanent Collection,* May 1–July 13, 1975.

Hudson Guild, New York, New York, *Rejoice—Art as Affirmation,* 1975.

Grey Art Gallery, New York University, New York, New York, *Inaugural Exhibition,* 1975.

Buecker and Harpsichords Gallery, New York, New York, *40 Years of American Collage,* January 3–January 28, 1976.

Lever House, New York, New York, *Group Show,* Organized by (but not exhibited at) Sculptor's Guild, New York, New York, October 22–November 18, 1976.

Pleiades Gallery, New York, New York, *Tenth Street Days, The Co-ops of the 50's,* December 20, 1976–January 7, 1977.

Westbeth Gallery, New York, New York, *American Abstract Artists,* 1976.

Storm King Art Center, Mountainville, New York, *Group Show: From The Collection,* September–October, 1977.

Solomon R. Guggenheim Museum, New York, New York, *From the American Collection,* September 30–November 13, 1977.

Buecker and Harpsichords Gallery, New York, New York, *Softworks/Fabric Pieces from the 60's,* November 5–December 24, 1977.

Truman Gallery, New York, New York, *Postcards and Other Mail,* December 13, 1977–January 7, 1978.

Landmark Gallery, New York, New York, *Tenth Street in 1977,* December 20, 1977–January 7, 1978.

Whitney Museum of American Art, New York, New York, *20th Century American Drawings: 5 Years of Acquisitions,* July 28–October 1, 1978. Catalogue.

Drew University College Art Gallery, Madison, New Jersey, *Reality In Art,* 1978.

Truman Gallery, New York, New York, *Five Artists,* 1978.

Freedman Gallery, Albright College, Reading, Pennsylvania, *Small is Beautiful,* February 8–March 4, 1979; Center Gallery, Buchnell University, Lewisburg, Pennsylvania, March 9–April 10, 1979.

Summit Art Center, Summit, New Jersey, *American Abstract Artists,* March 6–April 1, 1981.

Buecker and Harpsichords Gallery, New York, New York, *Sculptural Miniatures and Miniature Sculpture,* March 7–April 25, 1981.

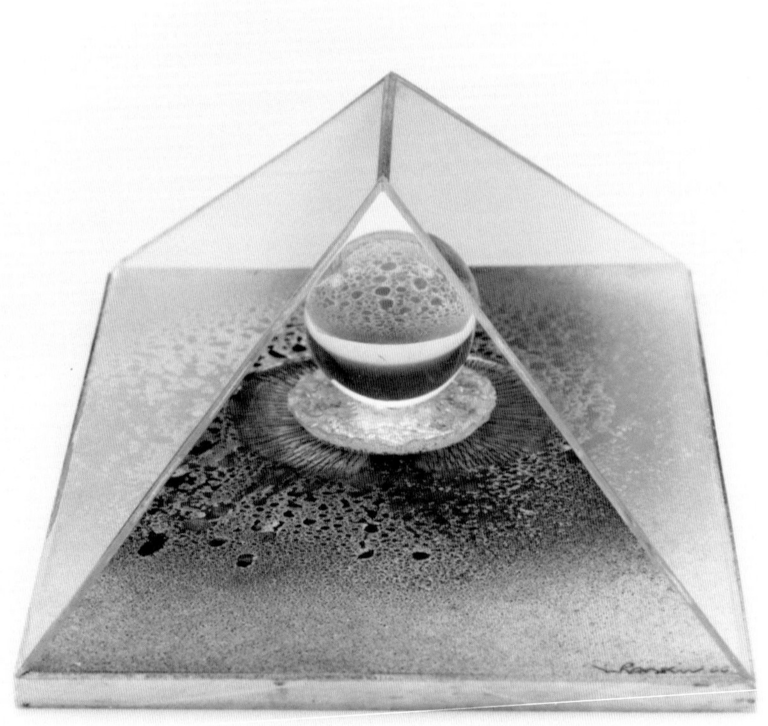

16 DRAWING FOR A TENT FLOOR, 1966
6 x 4¼ x 4¼

Bibliography

Articles and Exhibition Reviews (chronologically listed)

"Art of the Public [panel discussion]," *New York Times*, July 18, 1949.

Seckler, Dorothy. "At the Head of the Class," *Art News*, vol. 49, no. 5, September 1950, p. 50.

Mulligan, Charles M. *New York Post*, July 18, 1955, p. 12M.

O'Hara, Frank. *Arts Digest*, vol. 29, no. 20, September 15, 1955, p. 25.

M.S. *Art News*, vol. 54, no. 5, September 1955, p. 52.

"New Talent, Museum of Modern Art," *Newsday*, September 20, 1960, p. 37.

Genauer, Emily. "New Talent," *The New York Herald Tribune*, September 25, 1960, Section 4, p. 6.

Preston, Stuart. *New York Times*, September 25, 1960.

V.R. "New Talent," *Arts*, November 1960.

The Post and Times Star, [Cincinnati, Ohio], February 15, 1961, p. 42.

Yeiser, Frederick. "Watercolors," *The Cincinnati Enquirer*, February 19, 1961, Section C, p. 22.

Yeiser, Frederick. "Watercolors," *The Cincinnati Enquirer*, February 26, 1961, Section C, p. 4.

C.S.S. *Art News*, vol. 60, no. 2, April 1961, pp. 20 and 21.

C.S.S. *Arts*, April 1961.

The New York Herald Tribune, April 18, 1961, p. 34.

Preston, Stuart. *New York Times*, April 18, 1961, p. 34.

The Daily Intelligencer [Doylestown, Pennsylvania], July 10, 1961, p. 3.

The Villager [New York City], July 13, 1961.

Art News, vol. 60, no. 5, September 1961, p. 10.

The Cincinnati Israelite, September 7, 1961.

Oeri, Georgine. *Quadrum, Revue Internationale d'Art Moderne* [Brussels, Belgium], no. 11, 1961, pp. 154–155. Illus.

Art News, vol. 61, no. 2, April 1962, p. 18.

Pictures on Exhibit [New York City], March 1962, p. 25.

Polier, Betsy, *Manhattan East*, April 5, 1962, p. 5.

O'Doherty, Brian. *New York Times*, April 5, 1962.

France-Amérique, April 8, 1962, p. 15.

Parents Association of the High School of Music and Art. *Brush and Baton*, June 1962.

Preston, Stuart. *New York Times*, April 18, 1962, p. 34.

New York Journal American, April 31, 1962, p. 7.

New York Herald Tribune, September 16, 1962, Section 7, p. 15.

The Art Gallery [New York City], November 1962, p. 5 and 22.

Genauer, Emily. *New York Herald Tribune,* December 1, 1962, p. 7.

O'Doherty, Brian. *New York Times,* December 7, 1962

The Commercial Appeal [Memphis, Tennessee], December 16, 1962, Section 4, p. 8.

New York Herald Tribune [Paris], June 19, 1963, p. 5.

Electrical Merchandising Week, vol. 95, no. 29, July 22, 1963, p. 21. Cover.

Lerman, Leo. "Toys at Betty Parsons," *Grabbag* [New York City], December 1963.

"Silvermine Art Show," *New York Times,* June 17, 1964.

Hakanson, Joy. "Franklin Siden Gallery," *Detroit News,* July 8, 1964.

Bakalo, Helen. *Tanea (The News)* [Athens, Greece], January 22, 1965.

"14 American Watercolorists," *Swandesamitran* [Madras, India], March 27, 1965.

Lippard, Lucy. *Arts International,* vol. 9, no. 3, April 1965.

J.G. *Arts Magazine,* vol. 39, no. 7, April 1965, p. 57.

New York Arts Calendar [New York City], vol. 2, April 1965.

Preston, Stuart. *New York Times,* May 2, 1965.

"Trio of Watercolorists," *Detroit News,* June 20, 1965.

"Art in New York," *Time,* May 14, 1965.

J.B. *Arts Magazine,* vol. 39, no. 10, September–October 1965, p. 76.

Lippard, Lucy. *Arts International,* vol. 9, no. 6, September 1965, p. 60 and 66.

Canaday, John. *New York Times,* December 8, 1965.

Worth, Ian. *West Australian* [Perth], March 5, 1966.

"Die New Yorker Szene," *Das Kunstwerk* [Baden-Baden, West Germany], vol. 19, no. 10–2, April–June 1966, p. 2 and 26.

Chicago Midwest Art, vol. 2, no. 8, October 1966, p. 20.

Harkanson, Joy. *Detroit News,* October 2, 1966, p. 20.

Boostra, Rom. *Nieuwsblad van het Noorden van Zaterdag* [Holland], November 5, 1966, p. 27. Illus.

Roest, L. "Nederlandse Dagbladunie," *Het Vaderland* [Holland], November 1966. Illus.

Willard, Charlotte. *New York Post,* February 11, 1967, p. 46.

North-West Wind [Mount Kisco, New York], April 1967, pp. 4–7.

The Reporter Dispatch [White Plains, New York], May 11, 1967, p. 15.

The Reporter Dispatch [White Plains, New York], May 26, 1967, p. 25.

Kreisberg, Louisa. *The Reporter Dispatch* [White Plains, New York], May 27, 1967, p. 11.

New Yorker, June 1, 1967, p. 9.

Time, June 9, 1967, p. NY1 and 22.

Time, June 16, 1967, p. NY3.

Reif, Rita. *New York Times,* November 22, 1968, p. 55. Illus.

Adams, Alice. *Craft Horizons,* vol. 28, no. 6, November–December 1968, p. 36 and 56. Illus.

Wissis, Thomas. "Bringing the Art of Plastics Into Focus," *Chicago Tribune,* February 8, 1970.

Mellow, James R. "Brooklyn Museum Prints," *New York Times,* June 28, 1970.

New York Times, November 18, 1972, p. 4.

Senis, Harriet. *New York Post,* April 8, 1973.

"Observer-Tribune—Echoes Sentinel," *The Bernardsville News,* December 11, 1975, Section 2, p. 1.

Larsen, Susan C. *Arts Magazine,* vol. 52, no. 2, October 1977, p. 8. Illus.

Weintraub, Linda. *Philadelphia Arts Exchange,* January–February 1978, p. 53.

The New Yorker, March 27, 1978.

Zimmer, William. "Truman Gallery," *SoHo News* [New York City], April 1978.

Senis, Harriet. "Truman Gallery," *New York Post,* April 8, 1978.

Buonagurio, Edgar. *Arts Magazine,* vol. 52, no. 10, June 1978, p. 32. Illus.

Money, vol. 7, no. 8, August 1978, p. 48.

Collins, Nannie. *People Weekly,* vol. 10, no. 17, October 23, 1978, pp. 121–124.

Reif, Rita. *New York Times,* March 18, 1979, p. 33.

The Antique Trader Weekly [Dubuque, Iowa], June 4, 1979, p. 61.

Boston Sunday Globe, July 8, 1979, p. B2.

Tri-State Trader, July 14, 1979, p. 10.

Antique Monthly, August 1979, p. 7C.

Portfolio Magazine [New York City], vol. 1, no. 1, 1979.

Byers, Laura. *The Clarkon* [American Folk Art Museum], January 1980, p. 72.

Florescu, Michael. "From the Attic, From the Cellar—the Art of Leo Rabkin," *Arts,* October 1981.

Books (alphabetical by author)

American Abstract Artists. *American Abstract Artists 1936–1966,* New York: The Ram Press, 1966, Foreword and p. 5.

Benezit, E. *Dictionnaire des Peintres, Sculpteurs, Dessinateurs et Graveurs,* Paris, 1976, p. 567.

Bishop, Robert. *American Folk Sculpture,* New York: E.P. Dutton & Co., Inc., 1974, pp. 202, 327, 353, 364, 368, 370, 372–373, 374, and 380.

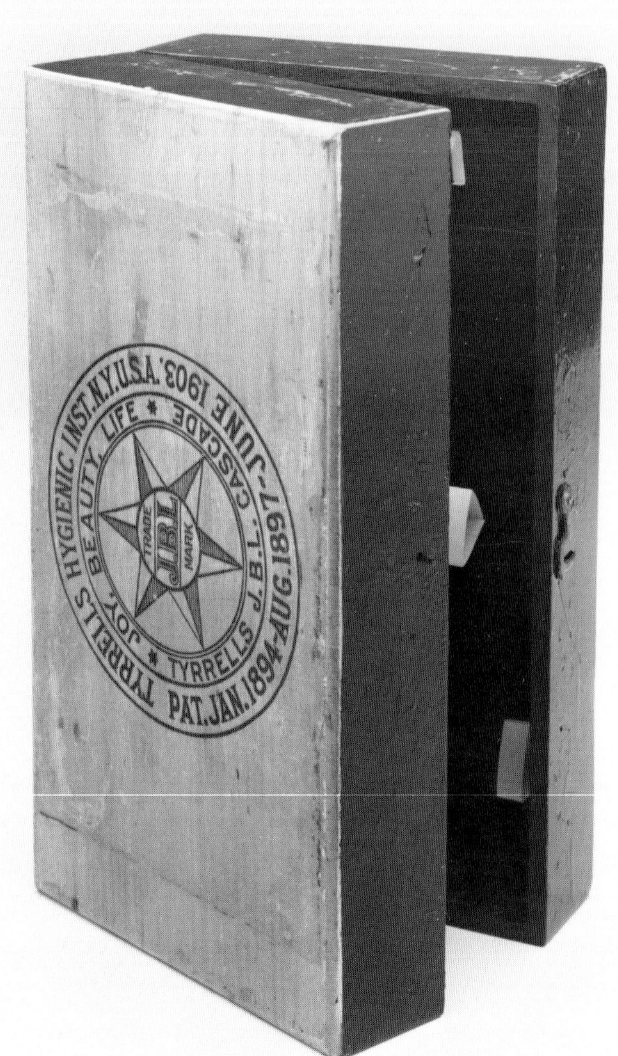
TYRRELLS HYGIENIC INST. N.Y. U.S.A.
PAT. JAN. 1894-AUG. 1897-JUNE 1903.
JOY, BEAUTY, LIFE *
CASCADE J.B.L. TYRRELLS *
TRADE
J.B.L.
MARK

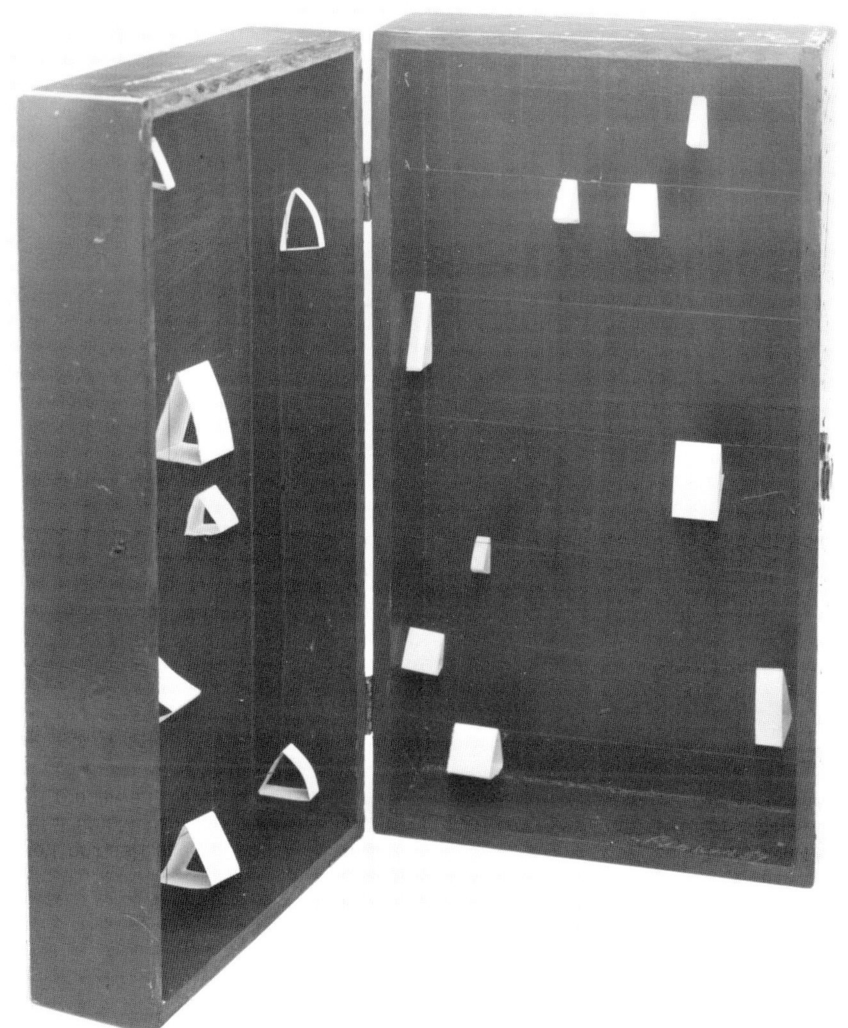

Bishop, Robert. *Treasure of American Folk Art,* New York: Harry N. Abrams, Inc., 1979, pp. 14–15.

Bunch, Clarence. *Acrylic for Sculpture and Design,* New York: Van Nostrand Reinhold Co., 1972, pp. 58–59 and 144.

Fox, Carl and H. Landshoff. *The Doll,* New York: Harry N. Abrams, Inc., 1974.

Johnson, Una E. *American Prints and Printmakers,* Garden City, New York: Doubleday & Co., 1980, pp. 162–163.

Larsen, Susan C. *American Abstract Artists—The Language of Abstraction,* Amherst, Massachusetts: Oxbow Press [distributed by Wittenborn & Co.], 1979.

Larsen, Susan C. *The American Abstract Artists Group: A History and Evaluation of Its Impact on American Art,* Doctoral Dissertation, Northwestern University, 1975.

Popper, Frank. *L'Art Cinétique,* Paris, 1970.

Sparks. *A Survey of Basic Mathematics,* New York: McGraw-Hill, 1971. Cover.

Who's Who in American Art, New York: Jacques Cattell Press, R. R. Bowker Co., 1973, p. 594; 1976, p. 453; 1978, p. 569; 1980, p. 603.

Who's Who in the East, Chicago: Marquis Who's Who, Inc., 1977–78, 1981.

La Jolla Museum of Contemporary Art

Board of Trustees

Staff

All color photographs and black-and-white photographs of works are by Jim Kiernan, New York. The catalogue was designed by Lilli Cristin, Glendale/Los Angeles and composed in Helvetica Light and Helvetica Bold faces by RS Typographics, North Hollywood. 1000 copies were lithographed on Quintessence Text and Kromekote Cover by Spectrum Printing, San Diego.